The Elements of C++ Style

The Elements of C++ Style is for all C++ practitioners, especially those working in teams where consistency is critical. Just as Strunk and White's *The Elements of Style* provides rules of usage for writing in the English language, this text furnishes a set of rules for writing in C++. The authors offer a collection of standards and guidelines for creating solid C++ code that will be easy to understand, enhance, and maintain.

This book provides conventions for

- formatting
- naming
- documentation
- programming
- and packaging

Trevor Misfeldt developed C++ and Java libraries at Rogue Wave Software for many years. He is currently CEO of CenterSpace Software, a developer of numerical libraries for the .NET platform. He is a co-author of *Elements of Java Style*.

Gregory Bumgardner has 24 years of software development experience, including 11 years of development in C++. He spent most of the past 10 years developing C++ libraries for Rogue Wave Software. He is currently working as an independent software consultant. He is a co-author of *Elements of Java Style*.

Andrew Gray is Director of Engineering for IntelliChem, a leading provider of software solutions for scientists. He was previously Software Engineering Manager and Technology Evangelist at Rogue Wave Software and has many years of experience developing applications in C++.

The Elements
of
C++ *Style*

Trevor Misfeldt
CenterSpace Software
Gregory Bumgardner
Freelance Consultant
Andrew Gray
IntelliChem Inc.

CAMBRIDGE
UNIVERSITY PRESS

PUBLISHED BY THE PRESS SYNDICATE OF THE UNIVERSITY OF CAMBRIDGE
The Pitt Building, Trumpington Street, Cambridge, United Kingdom

CAMBRIDGE UNIVERSITY PRESS
The Edinburgh Building, Cambridge CB2 2RU, UK
40 West 20th Street, New York, NY 10011-4211, USA
477 Williamstown Road, Port Melbourne, VIC 3207, Australia
Ruiz de Alarcón 13, 28014 Madrid, Spain
Dock House, The Waterfront, Cape Town 8001, South Africa

http://www.cambridge.org

First published 2004

Printed in the United States of America

Typefaces Adobe Garamond 10.5/12 pt. and ITC Avant Garde
System LaTeX 2_ε [TB]

A catalog record for this book is available from the British Library.

Library of Congress Cataloging in Publication Data
The elements of C++ style / Trevor Misfeldt [et al.].
      p.   cm.
   Includes bibliographical references and index.
   ISBN 0-521-89308-9 (pbk.)
   1. C++ (Computer program language)   I. Misfeldt, Trevor, 1969–
QA76.73.C153E28   2004
005.13′3 – dc22   2003061316

ISBN 0 521 89308 9 paperback

Contents

Preface

As commercial developers of software components, we always strive to have good, consistent style throughout our code. Since source code is usually included in our final products, our users often study our code to learn not just how the components work, but also how to write good software.

This fact ultimately led to the creation of a style guide for Java™ programming, entitled *The Elements of Java Style*.[1] The positive reception to that book, coupled with recurring questions about C++ style issues, resulted in this edition for C++.

If you've read *The Elements of Java Style* (or even if you haven't), much of the advice in this book will probably be familiar. This is deliberate, as many of the programming principles described are timeless and valid across programming languages. However, the content has been reworked and expanded here to address the unique characteristics of the C++ language.

Audience

We wrote this book for anyone writing C++ code, but especially for programmers who are writing C++ as part of a team. For a team to be effective, everyone must be able to read and understand everyone else's code. Having consistent style conventions is a good first step!

---

[1] Al Vermeulen, Jim Shur, Eldon Metz, Scott Ambler, Greg Bumgardner, Patrick Thompson and Trevor Misfeldt. *The Elements of Java Style*. (Cambridge, UK: Cambridge University Press, 2000).

This book is not intended to teach you C++, but rather it focuses on how C++ code can be written in order to maximize its effectiveness. We therefore assume you are already familiar with C++ and object-oriented programming. There are a number of good books about C++ basics; in particular, we recommend *The C++ Programming Language (3rd edition)* [2] and *The Design and Evolution of C++,* [3] both by Bjarne Stroustrup, the designer of the C++ language.

---

[2] Bjarne Stroustrup. *The C++ Programming Language, Third Edition.* (Reading, Massachusetts: Addison-Wesley, 1997).

[3] Bjarne Stroustrup. *The Design and Evolution of C++.* (Reading, Massachusetts: Addison-Wesley, 1994).

1.

Introduction

style: 1b. the shadow-producing pin of a sundial.
2c. -the custom or plan followed in spelling,
capitalization, punctuation, and typographic
arrangement and display.
                    —*Webster's New Collegiate Dictionary*

The syntax of a programming language tells you what code it is possible to write—what machines will understand. Style tells you what you ought to write—what humans reading the code will understand. Code written with a consistent, simple style is maintainable, robust, and contains fewer bugs. Code written with no regard to style contains more bugs, and may simply be thrown away and rewritten rather than maintained.

Attending to style is particularly important when developing as a team. Consistent style facilitates communication, because it enables team members to read and understand each other's work more easily. In our experience, the value of consistent programming style grows exponentially with the number of people working with the code.

Our favorite style guides are classics: Strunk and White's *The Elements of Style*[4] and Kernighan and Plauger's *The Elements of Programming Style*.[5] These small books work because they

---

[4] William Strunk, Jr., and E. B. White. *The Elements of Style, Fourth Edition.* (Allyn & Bacon, 2000).
[5] Brian Kernighan, and P. J. Plauger. *The Elements of Programming Style.* (New York: McGraw-Hill, 1988).

are simple: a list of rules, each containing a brief explanation and examples of correct, and sometimes incorrect, use. We followed the same pattern in this book. This simple treatment—a series of rules—enabled us to keep this book short and easy to understand.

Some of the advice that you read here may seem obvious to you, particularly if you've been writing code for a long time. Others may disagree with some of our specific suggestions about formatting or indentation. What we've tried to do here is distill many decades of experience into an easily accessible set of heuristics that encourage consistent coding practice (and hopefully help you avoid some C++ traps along the way). The idea is to provide a clear standard to follow so programmers can spend their time on solving the problems of their customers instead of worrying about things like naming conventions and formatting.

Disclaimer

We have dramatically simplified the code samples used in this book to highlight the concepts related to a particular rule. In many cases, these code fragments do not conform to conventions described elsewhere in this book—they lack real documentation and fail to meet certain minimum declarative requirements. Do not treat these fragments as definitive examples of real code!

Acknowledgments

Books like these are necessarily a team effort. Major contributions came from the original authors of *The Elements of Java Style*: Al Vermeulen, Scott Ambler, Greg Bumgardner, Eldon Metz, Trevor Misfeldt, Jim Shur, and Patrick Thompson. Both that book and this one have some roots in "C++

Design, Implementation, and Style Guide," written by Tom Keffer, and the "Rogue Wave Java Style Guide," and the "Ambysoft Inc. Coding Standards for Java," documents to which Jeremy Smith, Tom Keffer, Wayne Gramlich, Pete Handsman, and Cris Perdue all contributed. We'd also like to thank our former colleagues at Rogue Wave Software, from whom we've learned a lot over the years, and who have thus contributed to this work in both tangible and intangible ways.

Thanks also to the reviewers who provided valuable feedback on drafts of this book, including Ken Baldwin, Brand Hunt, Jim Shur, and Steve Sneller.

This book would certainly never have happened without the help and encouragement of the folks at Cambridge University Press, particularly Lara Zoble, who kept us on track throughout the writing and publication process.

2.

General Principles

While it is important to write software that performs well, many other issues should concern the professional developer. All *good* software performs well. But *great* software, written with style, is predictable, robust, maintainable, supportable, and extensible.

1. Adhere to the Style of the Original

When modifying existing software, your changes should follow the style of the original code.[6] Do not introduce a new coding style in a modification, and do not attempt to rewrite the old software just to make it match the new style. The use of different styles within a single source file produces code that is more difficult to read and comprehend. Rewriting old code simply to change its style may result in the introduction of costly yet avoidable defects.

2. Adhere to the Principle of Least Astonishment

The *Principle of Least Astonishment* suggests you should avoid doing things that would surprise a user of your software. This implies that the means of interaction and the behavior exhibited by your software must be predictable and consistent,[7] and,

---

[6] Jim Karabatsos. "When does this document apply?" In "Visual Basic Programming Standards." (GUI Computing Ltd., 22 March 1996.)
[7] George Brackett. "Class 6: Designing for Communication: Layout, Structure, Navigation for Nets and Webs." In "Course T525: Designing Educational Experiences for Networks and Webs." (Harvard Graduate School of Education, 26 August 1999.)

if not, the documentation must clearly identify and justify any unusual patterns of use or behavior.

To minimize the chances that a user would encounter something surprising in your software, you should emphasize the following characteristics in the design, implementation, packaging, and documentation of your C++ software:

Simplicity	Build simple classes and simple methods. Determine how much you need to do to meet the expectations of your users.
Clarity	Ensure that each class, interface, method, variable, and object has a clear purpose. Explain where, when, why, and how to use each.
Completeness	Provide the minimum functionality that any reasonable user would expect to find and use. Create complete documentation; document all features and functionality.
Consistency	Similar entities should look and behave the same; dissimilar entities should look and behave differently. Create and apply standards whenever possible.
Robustness	Provide predictable, documented behavior in response to errors and exceptions. Do not hide errors and do not force clients to detect errors.

3. Do It Right the First Time

Apply these rules to any code you write, not just code destined for production. More often than not, some piece of prototype or experimental code will make its way into a finished product, so you should anticipate this eventuality. Even if your code never makes it into production, someone else may still have to read it. Anyone who must look at your code will appreciate your professionalism and foresight at having consistently applied these rules from the start.

4. *Document any Deviations*

No standard is perfect and no standard is universally applicable. Sometimes you will find yourself in a situation where you need to deviate from an established standard.

Before you decide to ignore a rule, you should first make sure you understand why the rule exists and what the consequences are if it is not applied. If you decide you must violate a rule, then document why you have done so.

This is the *prime directive.*

3.

Formatting

Conventions

3.1 Indentation

If you are managing a development team, do not leave it up to individual developers to choose their own indentation amount and style. Establish a standard indentation policy for the organization and ensure that everyone complies with this standard.

Our recommendation of two spaces appears to be the most common standard, although your organization may prefer three or even four spaces.

5. Use Indented Block Statements

One way to improve code readability is to group individual statements into block statements and uniformly indent the content of each block to set off its contents from the surrounding code.

If you generate code using a C++ development environment, use the indentation style produced by the environment. If you are generating the code by hand, use two spaces to ensure readability without taking up too much space:

```
DNode::DNode(DNode *prev, DNode *next) {
··if (0 != next) {
····next->prev_ = this;
··}
```

```
··if (0 != prev) {
····prev->next_ = this;
··}
··next_ = next;
··prev_ = prev;
}
```

6. *Indent Statements after a Label*

In addition to indenting the contents of block statements, you should also indent the statements that follow a label to make the label easier to notice:

```
void Foo::doSomething(int arg) {
··loop:
····for (int index = 0; index <= arg; index++) {
······switch (index) {
········case 0:
··········// ...
··········break; // exit the switch statement
········default:
··········// ...
··········break; // exit the switch statement
······}
····}
}
```

7. *Choose One Style for Brace Placement*

You have two choices for placing the opening brace of a block statement: you may place the brace at the end of the line that controls entry into the block, or you may place it on the next line and align it with the first character of the first line. You should always place the closing brace on a line of its own and align it with the first character of the line containing the opening brace:

```
void sameLine() {
}

void nextLine()
{
}
```

While many programmers use one or both of these styles, your organization should choose one style and apply it consistently.

In this book, we use the first style of brace placement. The following examples illustrate how this rule applies to each of the various C++ definition and control constructs.

Class definitions:

```
class Outer {
  public:
    Outer();
    class Inner {
      public:
        Inner();
    };
};
```

Function definitions:

```
void display() {
  // ...
}
```

For-loop statements:

```cpp
for (int i = 0; i <= j; i++) {
  // ...
}
```

If and else statements:

```cpp
if (j < 0) {
  // ...
}
else if (j > 0) {
  // ...
}
else {
  // ...
}
```

Try, catch blocks:

```cpp
try {
  // ...
}
catch (...) {
  // ...
}
```

Switch statements:

```cpp
switch (value) {
  case 0:
    // ...
    break;
  default:
    // ...
```

```
    break;
}
```

While statements:

```
while (++k <= j) {
  // ...
}
```

Do-while statements:

```
do {
  // ...
} while (++k <= j);
```

8. *Break Long Statements into Multiple Lines*

While a modern window-based editor can easily handle long source code lines by scrolling horizontally, a printer must truncate, wrap, or print on separate sheets any lines that exceed its maximum printable line width. To ensure your source code is still readable when printed, you should limit your source code line lengths to the maximum width your printing environment supports, typically 80 to 132 characters.

First, do not place multiple statement expressions on a single line if the result is a line that exceeds your maximum allowable line length. If two statement expressions are placed on one line,

```
double x = rand(); double y = rand(); // Too
Long!
```

then introduce a new line to place them on separate lines:

```
double x = rand();
double y = rand();
```

Second, if a line is too long because it contains a complex expression,

```
double length = sqrt(pow(rand(), 2.0) +
pow(rand(), 2.0)); // Too Long!
```

then subdivide the expression into several smaller subexpressions. Use a separate line to store the result produced by an evaluation of each subexpression into a temporary variable:

```
double xSquared = pow(rand(), 2.0);
double ySquared = pow(rand(), 2.0);
double length = sqrt(xSquared + ySquared);
```

Last, if a long line cannot be shortened under the preceding guidelines, then break, wrap, and indent that line using the following rules.

Step one:

If the top-level expression on the line contains one or more commas,

```
double length = sqrt(pow(x, 2.0), pow(y, 2.0));
// Too Long!
```

then introduce a line break after each comma. Align each expression following a comma with the first character of the expression preceding the comma:

```
double length = sqrt(pow(x, 2.0),
                     pow(y, 2.0));
```

Step two:

If the top-level expression on the line contains no commas,

```
return person1.getName() == person2.getName() &&
person1.getAddress() == person2.getAddress();
// Too Long!
```

then introduce a line break just before the operator with the lowest precedence; or, if more than one operator of equally low precedence exists between each such operator,

```
return person1.getName() == person2.getName() &&
       person1.getAge() == person2.getAge();
```

Step three:

Reapply steps one and two, as required, until each line created from the original statement expression is less than the maximum allowable length.

9. Include White Space

White space is the area on a page devoid of visible characters. Code with too little white space is difficult to read and understand, so use plenty of white space to delineate methods, comments, code blocks, and expressions clearly.

Use a single space to separate the keywords, parentheses, and curly braces in conditional statements:

```
for·(...)·{
  //...
}
```

```cpp
while (...) {
  // ...
}

do {
  // ...
} while (...);

switch (...) {
  // ...
}

if (...) {
  // ...
}
else if (...) {
  // ...
}
else {
  // ...
}

try {
  // ...
}
catch (...) {
  // ...
}
```

Use a single space on either side of binary operators, except for the "." or "->" operators:

```cpp
double length = sqrt(x * x + y * y);
double xNorm = length > 0.0 ? (x / length) : x;
double height = person.getHeight();
```

Use blank lines to separate each logical section of a method implementation:

```
void handleMessage(const Message& messsage){

  DataInput content = message.getDataInput();
  int messageType = content.readInt();

  switch (messageType) {

    case WARNING:
      // ... do some stuff here ...
      break;

    case ERROR:
      // ... do some stuff here ...
      break;

    default:
      // ... do some stuff here ...
      break;
  }
}
```

Use blank lines to separate each function definition in a source file:

```
std::string Customer::getName(void) const {
  // ...
}

void Customer::setName(std::string) {
  // ...
}
```

10. Do Not Use "Hard" Tabs

Many developers use tab characters to indent and align their source code without realizing that the interpretation of tab characters varies across environments. Code that appears to possess the correct formatting when viewed in the original editing environment can appear unformatted and virtually unreadable when viewed by another developer or transported to an environment that interprets tabs differently.

To avoid this problem, always use spaces instead of tabs to indent and align source code. You may do this simply by using the space bar instead of the tab key or by configuring your editor to replace tabs with spaces. Some editors also provide a "smart" indentation capability. You should disable this feature if it uses tab characters.

4.

Naming

Conventions

Consistent use of naming conventions can provide visual cues to a given identifier's role.

4.1 Preprocessor Macro Names

11. *Use UPPERCASE and Underscores for Preprocessor Macro Names*

The capitalization of preprocessor names distinguishes them from symbols defined using C++ grammar:

```
#define DEPRECATED_FEATURE
#define MIN(a,b) ((a) < (b) ? (a) : (b))
```

12. *Add a Unique Prefix to Macro Names*

Add a prefix to macro names to create names that will not conflict with those defined in user or third-party software. We recommend that you add an abbreviation that identifies your organization and, optionally, an abbreviation that identifies your product: i.e., ACME_DB_TRACE.

The preferred approach to avoiding naming conflicts is to declare all identifiers within a class or namespace, as described in Rules 79 and 80.

4.2 Type and Constant Names

13. *Use "UpperCamelCase" for Classes, Constants, Structures, Enumerations, and Typedefs*

Capitalize the first letter of each word that appears in a type name or constant name to provide a visual cue for separating the individual words within a name. The leading capital letter provides a mechanism for differentiating between types and variables or functions (see Rules 16 and 19):

```
enum BackgroundColor {
  None,
  Red,
  Green,
  Blue
};

const int FixedWidth = 10;

class BankAccount {
  // ...
};


typedef list<BankAccount> Portfolio;
```

14. *Use Nouns to Name Compound Types*

Classes, structs, or typedefs that define objects, or things, should be identified by nouns:

```
class Customer {
  // ...
};

typedef int Dollars;
```

15. *Pluralize the Names of Collections*

Collections of objects should have a name that corresponds to the plural form of the object type contained in the collection. This enables a reader of your code to distinguish between variables representing multiple values from those representing single values:

```
class Shapes {
  public:
    int getShape(int index);
    void removeShape(int index);
    void addShape(Shape shape);
    int getCount();
};


typedef list<Shape> Shapes;


Shape shapes[ShapeCount];
```

4.3 Function Names

16. *Use "lowerCamelCase" for Function Names*

Use lowercase for the first word and capitalize each subsequent word that appears in a function name to provide a visual cue for separating the individual words within each name.

The leading lowercase letter provides a mechanism for differentiating between functions and types:

```
class Customer {
  public:
    void setAddress(const Address& address);
};
```

17. Use Verbs to Name Functions

Functions commonly define *actions*, which are described by verbs:

```
class Account {
  public:
    void withdraw(int amount);
    void deposit(int amount);
};
```

18. Use "is", "set", and "get" to Name Accessor and Mutator Functions

Your classes should provide read access to Boolean members using functions that begin with the word "is":

```
bool Tool::isValid(void) const {
  return isValid_;
}
```

You should provide read access to other member types using functions that begin with the word "get":

```
string Tool::getName(void) const {
  return name_;
}
```

Similarly, you should provide read access to indexed members using a "get" function that takes a size_t index argument:

```
std::string Tool::getAlias(size_t index)const {
  return aliases_[index];
}
```

You should provide write access to members using functions that begin with the word "set":

```
void Tool::setValid(bool isValid) {
  isValid_ = isValid;
}
```

```
void Tool::setName(const string& name) {
  name_ = name;
}
```

```
void Tool::setCode(size_t index, int code) {
  codes_[index] = code;
}
```

4.4 Variable and Parameter Names

19. Use "lowerCamelCase" for Variable and Function Parameter Names

Use lowercase for the first word and capitalize each subsequent word that appears in a variable name to provide a visual cue for separating the individual words within each name.

```
class Customer {
  public:
    Address setAddress(const Address& address);
  private:
    Address address_;
};
```

```
Address Customer::setAddress(Address address) {
  Address oldAddress = address_;
```

```
  address_ = address;
  return oldAddress;
}
```

The leading lowercase letter provides a mechanism for differentiating between variables and constants:

```
const int ConstantValue = 10;
int variableValue = 1;
```

20. Use Nouns to Name Variables

Variables refer to objects or things, which are described by nouns. Pluralize variables that identify collections:

```
class Customer {
  private:
    Address billingAddress_;
    Address shippingAddress_;
    Phone daytimePhone_;
    Orders openOrders_;
};
```

21. Add a Prefix or Suffix to Member Variable Names to Distinguish Them from Other Variables

Adopt this practice to reduce the potential for accidental name-hiding and to improve the readability of your code. Choose one style and use it consistently throughout your product. If you are extending or working within a third-party framework, use the same style as the framework, if one exists:

```
class Customer {
  private:
    Address home_; // Style used in this book
```

```
    Address m_work; // Style used in MFC code
};
```

22. *Name All Function Parameters*

Supply the same meaningful name for each function parameter in both the function declaration and the function definition. If the function makes no use of the parameter, use
static_cast<> to recast the parameter variable as type void
to eliminate any "unused variable" compiler warning. An alter-
native approach for handling unused parameters is described
in Rule 144.

When declaring functions that take no arguments use a pair
of parentheses containing the keyword void:

```
class MyClass {
  public:
    MyClass(void);                   // OK
    MyClass(int);                    // Bad
    MyClass(float meaningfulName);   // Good
    void method1(void);              // Consistent
    void method2();                  // Inconsistent
};


MyClass::MyClass(int){               // Bad
  // ...
}


MyClass::MyClass(float meaningfulName) {
  static_cast<void>(meaningfulName); // Good
  // ...
}
```

23. *Use "other" for Parameter Names in Copy Constructors and Assignment Operators*

Choose a naming convention for the parameter name used in copy constructors and assignment operators. We use other throughout this book:

```
class A {
  A(const A& other);
  A& operator=(const A& other);
};
```

You might instead choose to use the lowerCamelCase name of the class or the word "that".

24. *Give Function Parameters the Same Name as the Member Variables You Assigned Them to*

Naming function parameters after the member variables they correspond to provides a clue to the reader that the parameters are assigned to members:

```
class Customer {
  public:
    Customer(const string& name);
    void setName(const string& name);
  private:
    string name_;
};

Customer::Customer(const string& name)
  : name_(name) {
}

void Customer::setName(const string& name) {
  name_ = name;
}
```

4.5 General

25. *Use Meaningful Names*

Use names that are, and will remain, meaningful to those who will eventually read your code. Use meaningful words to create names. Avoid using a single character or generic names that do little to define the purpose of the entities they name.

The purpose for the variable "a" and the constant "65" in the following code is unclear:

```
if (a < 65) {// What property does 'a' describe?
  y = 65 - a;// What is being calculated here?
}
else {
  y = 0;
}
```

The code is much easier to understand when meaningful names are used:

```
if (age < RetirementAge) {
  yearsToRetirement = RetirementAge - age;
}
else {
  yearsToRetirement = 0;
}
```

The only exception to this rule concerns temporary variables whose context provides sufficient information to determine their purpose, such as a variable used as a counter or index within a loop:

```
for (size_t i = 0; i < numberOfStudents; ++i) {
  enrollStudent(i);
}
```

26. Use Familiar Names

Use words that exist in the terminology of the target domain. If your users refer to "customers," then use the name `Customer` for the class, not `Client`. Many developers make the mistake of creating new or generic terms for concepts when satisfactory terms already exist in the target industry or domain.

27. Avoid the Use of Digits within Names

Avoid using numbers to distinguish names, such as `str1` and `str2`. You should use digits if they are necessary for the meaning of the identifier, e.g., `Utf16Encoding` to identify a standard Unicode encoding.

28. Avoid Excessively Long Names

The name given an object must adequately describe its purpose. If a class, interface, variable, or method has an overly long name, then that entity is probably trying to accomplish too much.

Instead of simply giving the entity a new name that conveys less meaning, first reconsider its design or purpose. A refactoring of the entity may produce new classes, interfaces, methods, or variables that are more focused and can be given more meaningful yet simpler names.

29. Join the Vowel Generation—Use Complete Words

Do not attempt to shorten names by removing vowels. This practice reduces the readability of your code and introduces ambiguity if more than one meaningful name reduces to the same consonants.

```
class Msg {                              // Bad!
  void appndSig(Msg msg, string sig); // Bad!
```

```
  void setSigMask(int mask) const;      // Bad!
};
```

The casual reader can understand the names in this definition:

```
class Message {
  void appendSignature(Message message, string
signature);
  void setSignalMask(int mask) const;
};
```

If you find yourself removing vowels simply to shorten a long name, then you need to question whether the original name is appropriate (see the preceding rule).

30. Use "lowerCamelCase" for Abbreviations

If an abbreviation appears as the first word in a type or constant, only capitalize the first letter of the abbreviation.

Use this style to eliminate confusion in names where uppercase letters act as word separators. This is especially important if one abbreviation immediately follows another:

```
XMLString          > XmlString
loadXMLDocument()  > loadXmlDocument()
```

This rule does not apply to abbreviations that appear within the name of a preprocessor constant because these names only contain capital letters (see Rule 11):

```
#define XML_DOCUMENT = "text/XML";
```

The rule does not apply to abbreviations that appear at the beginning of a function, variable, or parameter name because these names should always start with a lowercase letter:

```
Document xmlDocument;
```

31. Do Not Use Case to Differentiate Names

C++ compilers can distinguish between names that differ only in case, but a human reader may fail to notice the difference. This is equivalent to name-hiding.

For example, do not name a class `XmlStream` if a class named `XMLStream` already exists. If both names appear in the same scope, each effectively hides the other when considered from the perspective of a person trying to read and understand the code.

5.

Documentation

Conventions

Developers often forget that the primary purpose of their software is to satisfy the needs of an end user; they often concentrate on the solution but fail to instruct others on the use of that solution.

Good software documentation not only tells others how to use your software, it also acts as a specification of interfaces and behaviors for the engineers who must help you develop the software and those who will later maintain and enhance it. While you should always make every attempt to write software that is self-explanatory, your end users may not have access to the source code; there will always be significant information about usage and behavior that a programming language cannot express.

Good programmers enjoy writing documentation. Like elegant design and implementation, good documentation is a sign of a professional programmer.

32. *Document Your Software Interface for Those Who Must Use It*

Document the public interface of your code so others can understand and use it correctly and effectively.

The primary purpose for documentation comments is to define a *programming contract* [8] between a *client* and a supplier of a *service*. The documentation associated with a method should describe all aspects of behavior on which a caller of that method can rely and should not attempt to describe implementation details.

Describe each C++ element that appears in, or forms part of, the interface.

33. Document Your Implementation for Those Who Must Maintain It

Document the implementation of your code so others can maintain and enhance it. Always assume that someone who is completely unfamiliar with your code will eventually have to read and understand it.

34. Keep Your Comments and Code Synchronized

> When the code and the comments disagree, both are probably wrong.
>
> —*Norm Schryer, Bell Labs*

When you modify code, make sure you also update any related comments. The code and documentation together form a software product, so treat each with equal importance.

35. Embed Application Program Interface (API) Reference Documentation in Your Source Code

Embed your software reference documentation in your source files so they can be easily updated any time changes are made to the code. By embedding the documentation in the code, you also assist those who must understand and maintain your

---

[8] Brian Kernighan, and P. J. Plauger. *The Elements of Programming Style.* (New York: McGraw-Hill, 1988), p. 118.

code, since they do not have to locate and update externally maintained documentation.

36. Generate API Reference Documentation Directly from the Source Code

Use a C++ documentation tool[9] to extract comments and declarations to create API reference documentation. Automatically generated documentation is typically more accurate, complete, and up-to-date than externally maintained documentation. Choose a tool that can index and cross-reference your software even if the code does not yet contain documentation comments.

37. Document All Significant Software Elements

Document every namespace, structure, union, class, member function, member variable, global function, global variable, and macro that appears in an API. Document both public and private members (see Rules 32 and 33). Code contained in a source file is no less deserving of documentation than that contained in public header files.

While this level of detail may seem excessive, it should be obvious that too much documentation is almost always better than too little. Eventually someone will appreciate your efforts and that person might be you.

38. Document Software Elements as Early as Possible

Document each software element before or during its implementation; do not delay until the project is nearing completion. Documentation generated at the end of a project often lacks detail because the authors have become too familiar or too bored with the code.

---

[9] See http://www.literateprogramming.com/ for an extensive list of documentation tools. We have used the tool *doxygen*, by Dimitri van Heesch (www.doxygen.org), with some success.

If you create software reference documentation prior to implementation, you can use this documentation to define requirements for the developers assigned to implement the software.

39. Use Block Comments to Describe the Programming Interface

Describe the purpose and usage of each interface element in a comment block immediately preceding the declaration of that element. If using an automatic documentation extraction tool, use the comment block format required by that tool.

40. Use One-Line Comments to Explain Implementation Details

Use one or more one-line comments to document

- The purpose of specific variables or expressions.
- Any implementation-level design decisions.
- The source material for complex algorithms.
- Defect fixes or workarounds.
- Code that may benefit from further optimization or elaboration.
- Any known problems, limitations, or deficiencies.

Strive to minimize the need for embedded comments by writing code that documents itself. Do not add comments that simply repeat what the code does. Add comments only if they add useful information:

```
// Calculate discount before printing the total.
if (invoiceTotal > DiscountThreshold) {

   // The discount is hard-coded because current
   // customers all use the same discount rate.
   // We will need to replace this constant with
   // a variable if we ever get a customer who
```

```
// needs a different rate, or one that wants
// to apply multiple discount rates!

invoiceTotal *= Discount;
}
```

41. Use a Single Consistent Format and Organization for All Documentation Comments

Each software element that appears in an API possesses characteristics that may have significance for users. Standardize upon a set of characteristics that must be documented for each type of software element. Specify the order in which the descriptions of these characteristics should appear within the documentation block. Indicate which descriptions are required and which are optional. Specify the handling of inapplicable characteristics.

42. Provide a Summary Description of Every Declared Element

All documentation blocks should begin with a single sentence, summary description of the associated software element:

```
// This method reads the current temperature
// from the probe, in degrees Celsius.
```

If the summary fails to describe all aspects of the purpose and usage of the element, expand upon the summary description in subsequent paragraphs.

43. Document the Interface Exposed by Every Function

Function documentation should include descriptions of each parameter, the return value, and any exceptions thrown by that function. If the function reports an error via an indirect mechanism, such as `errno()`, specify the error query method, the list of possible errors, and the lifespan of the error indication:

```
/*
 *...
 * Parameters:
 *    probe  the probe number to read
 * Returns: the current temperature, in Celsius
 * Throws:  InstrumentationException if the
 *          probe does not respond.
 *...
 */
double getTemperature(size_t probe);
```

Macro documentation should include descriptions of each parameter and how they affect resulting expansion of the macro.

44. Document Thread Synchronization Requirements

If a class or method might be used in a multithreaded environment, document the level of thread safety provided. Indicate whether the object may be shared between threads and, if so, whether it requires external synchronization to enforce serialized access. A fully thread-safe object or function uses its own synchronization mechanism to protect internal state in the presence of multiple threads. See also Rule 64.

45. Provide Examples to Illustrate Common and Proper Usage

When the purpose or usage of a class, function, or macro is not obvious, provide usage examples. If possible, extract examples from example programs that compile and execute without error.

46. Document Important Preconditions, Postconditions, and Invariant Conditions

A *precondition* is a condition that must hold true before a method starts if this method is to behave properly. A typical precondition may limit the range of acceptable values for a method parameter.

A *postcondition* is a condition that must hold true following the completion of a method if this method has behaved properly. A typical postcondition describes the state of an object that should result from an invocation of the method given an initial state and the invocation arguments.

An *invariant* is a condition that must always hold true for an object. A typical invariant might restrict an integer field representing the current month to a value between 1 and 12.

Documenting preconditions, postconditions, and invariants is important because these define the assumptions under which users interact with a class. For example, if a method allocates resources that must be released by the caller, then this should be clearly documented. (Of course, this isn't necessarily good practice; see Rule 156.)

See also Rules 59 and 152.

47. Document Known Defects and Deficiencies

Identify and describe any outstanding problems associated with a class or method. Indicate any replacements or work-arounds that exist. If possible, indicate when the problem might be resolved.

While no one likes to publicize problems in his or her code, your colleagues and customers will appreciate the information. This information gives them the chance to implement a workaround or to isolate the problem to minimize the impact of future changes.

48. Use the Active Voice to Describe Actors and Passive Voice to Describe Actions

In English prose, the active voice is normally preferred over the passive voice. However, this is not always the case in technical documentation. This is especially true when a document provides usage instructions.

Use the active voice when the actor in a situation is important.

Prefer:

- *A* Time *object represents a point in time.*
- *Use* time() *to get the current system time.*

Avoid:

- *A point in time is represented by a* Time *object.*
- *The system time is returned by* time().

Use the passive voice when the object being acted upon or the action is important but the actor is not:

- *The* Guard *object is destroyed upon exit from the enclosing block scope.*
- *The* reset() *method must be called prior to invoking any other method.*

You may choose to treat a software element as the implied subject in single-sentence, synoptic descriptions of that element:

[time()] Returns the current time.

However, do not use this grammatical style in the main body of the element description. Use complete sentences that identify the element by name or "this" instead:

- *The* time() *method ignores time zones.*
- *This method ignores time zones.*

49. Use "this" Rather Than "the" When Referring to Instances of the Current Class

When describing the purpose or behavior of a method, use "`this`" instead of "the" to refer to an object that is an instance of the class defining the method:

```
/**
 * Returns the string value of this object.
 */
std::string toString();
```

50. Explain Why the Code Does What It Does

Good code is self-documenting. Another developer should be able to look at well-written code and determine *what* it does; however, he or she may not know *why* it does it.

The comments in the following code provide little additional information:

```
// Divide the vector components by the
// vector length.
double length = 0;
for (size_t i = 0; i < vectorCount; i++) {
    double x = vector[i].x;
    double y = vector[i].y;
    length = sqrt(x * x, y * y);
    vector[i].x = vector[i].x / length;
    vector[i].y = vector[i].y / length;
}
```

After reading this code, a reasonable developer may still not understand what or why this code does what it does. Use internal comments to provide this information:

```
// Normalize each vector to produce a unit
// vector that can be used as a direction
```

```cpp
// vector in geometry calculations and
// transformations.

double length = 0;
for (size_t i = 0; i < vectorCount; i++) {
  double x = vector[i].x;
  double y = vector[i].y;
  length = sqrt(x * x, y * y);
  // Normalize the vector to produce a
  // unit vector.
  vector[i].x = vector[i].x / length;
  vector[i].y = vector[i].y / length;
}
```

51. *Avoid the Use of End-Line Comments*

Avoid adding comments to the end of a line of code. Such comments can easily interfere with the visual structure of code. Modifications to a commented line of code may push the comment far enough to the right that it cannot be seen in a text editor. Some programmers try to improve the appearance of end-line comments by aligning them so they are left justified. If this appearance is to be maintained, the comments must be realigned each time the code is modified.

Place one-line comments on a separate line immediately preceding the code to which they refer. There are exceptions to this rule, such as when a comment labels a line of code to identify changes or to support search and replace operations. End-of-line comments may also be used to describe simple local variables or to label highly nested control structures (see next rule).

52. *Label Closing Braces in Highly Nested Control Structures*

While you should generally avoid creating deeply nested control structures, you can improve the readability of such code by adding end-line comments to the closing braces of each structure:

```c
for (size_t i; ...) {
  for (size_t j; ...) {
    while (!done) {
      if (...) {
        switch (...) {
          // ...
        } // end switch
      } // end if
    } // end while
  } // end for j
} // end for i
```

53. *Add a "fall-through" Comment between Two* case *Labels if no* break *Statement Separates Those Labels*

When the code following a switch statement's case label does not include a break but instead "falls through" into the code associated with the next label, add a comment to indicate this was your intent. Other developers may either incorrectly assume a break occurs, or wonder whether you simply forgot to code one:

```c
switch (command) {
  case FastForward:
    isFastForward = true;
    // Fall through!
  case Play:
  case Forward:
    isForward = true;
    break;
  case FastRewind:
    isFastRewind = true;
    // Fall through!
```

```
  case Rewind:
    isRewind = true;
    break;
    // ...
}
```

Note that two adjacent labels do not require an intervening comment.

54. Use Keywords to Mark Pending Work, Unresolved Issues, Defects, and Bug Fixes

Establish a set of keywords or tags for use in creating special comments that you and other developers can use to mark and locate important sections of code. These flags are especially useful in marking sections of code that are known to be incomplete or incorrect or require further inspection.

Keywords used to label unresolved issues should include the name or initials of the person who raised the issue and the date that this person identified or resolved the issue. Choose keyword strings that are unlikely to appear anywhere else in the code:

```
// **FIX** #1234 - Added code to flush buffer.

// :UNRESOLVED: Greg B., 2002/11/19
// This code does not handle the case where
// the input overflows the internal buffer!!
while (everMoreInput) {

   ...

}
```

6.

Programming

Principles

A complete treatment of programming principles and software design is clearly beyond the scope of this book. However, this chapter includes some core principles that we have found to be central to good software engineering.

6.1 Engineering

55. *Do Not be Afraid to Do Engineering*

The ultimate goal of professional software development is to create something useful—an engineering task much more than a scientific one. (Science is more immediately concerned with understanding the world around us, which is admittedly necessary, but not sufficient, for engineering.)

Resist the temptation to write code to model scientific realities that include all theoretical possibilities. It is not a "hack" to write code that has practical limitations if you are confident those limits do not affect the utility of the resulting system.

For example, imagine you need a data structure for tree traversal and choose to write a stack. The stack needs to hold at least as many items as the maximum depth of any tree. Now suppose that there is no theoretical limit to how deep one of these trees can be. You might be tempted to create a stack that can grow to an arbitrary size by reallocating memory and copying its items as needed. On the other hand, your team's understanding of the application may be such that in your wildest imagination you'd be amazed to see a tree with depth greater than 10. If so, the better choice would be to create a fixed-length stack with a maximum of, say, 50 elements.

You might hear a little voice complain, "There is still a chance greater than zero that a tree will come along with 51 elements and my application will fail, therefore my code is wrong." Be assured, if you write the more complex class to handle any eventuality, there is a much larger chance that your application will fail due to a programming error, unexpected side effects, or misunderstanding of the class's semantics.

This said, it is also important to document any assumptions that you're making and any practical limitations you're aware of. It is very realistic that someone needing a stack will come along later and decide to make use of the one you've already written, but 50 elements might not be a reasonable number of items for that one. This documentation should appear directly in the code, as well as any technical documentation that accompanies the system.

56. *Choose Simplicity over Elegance*

Strive for elegance in designs and code, but sometimes it is better to stop short of the most elegant solution in favor of a simpler one. While elegant solutions often have an element of simplicity, it is not always the case that simple solutions are elegant. There is nothing particularly elegant about a 50-line sequence of `if-else` statements, but if it is the simplest most straightforward approach to the problem, there is no reason to try and turn it into something it does not need to be.

57. Do Not Use a Feature of C++ just "because it is there"

C++ is not Mount Everest, so, with all due respect to Sir Edmund Hillary, do not use a feature of C++ "because it is there."

The richness of C++ is both a strength and a weakness. While every feature of the C++ language is there for a reason, use the guidelines in this book and the collective wisdom of the C++ community to be sure you use those features appropriately. Misuse of features such as templates, RTTI, namespaces, preprocessing, operator overloading, exception handling, multiple inheritance, and the rest can quickly result in less robust, less maintainable code.

For a great deal of insight into the design decisions that influenced C++ language features, please see Stroustrup's *The Design and Evolution of C++.*[10]

58. Recognize the Cost of Reuse

Reuse is often held up as the holy grail of object-oriented programming and, indeed, reuse is a wonderful thing for obvious reasons. But do not overlook the costs such as increased dependencies and complexity, which can sometimes outweigh any benefits.

Reusable components are notoriously hard to build and maintain. A designer has to anticipate a wide variety of usage scenarios. Once they are in use, maintenance becomes very difficult due largely to backwards compatibility issues. The assumption that components should be reusable by default also puts stress on development organizations because it forces increased

---

[10] Bjarne Stroustrup. *The Design and Evolution of C++.* (Reading, Massachusetts: Addison-Wesley, 1994).

coordination between different groups. More users leads to increased complexity which leads to higher costs.

59. Program by Contract

A method is a contract[11] between a caller and a callee. The contract states the caller must abide by the preconditions of the method and the method, in turn, must return results that satisfy the postconditions associated with that method.

Abiding by the preconditions of a method usually means passing arguments as the method expects them; it may also mean calling a set of methods in the correct order. To abide by the postconditions of the method, the method must correctly complete the work it was called upon to perform and it must leave the object in a consistent state.

Check preconditions and postconditions by assertion (see Rule 152) in appropriate public methods. Check preconditions at the beginning of a method, before any other code is executed, and check postconditions at the end of a method before the method returns (see also Rule 46).

Derived classes that override superclass methods must preserve the pre- and postconditions of the superclass method. To ensure this, use the template method design pattern[12] by using public non-virtual methods to call protected virtual methods that provide the functional implementation. Each public method will test preconditions, call the associated virtual method, and then test postconditions. A subclass may override

---

[11] Bertrand Meyer. *Object-Oriented Software Construction, Second Edition.* (Englewood Cliffs, NJ: Prentice Hall, 2000).
[12] Erich Gamma, Richard Helm, Ralph Johnson, John Vlissides. *Design Patterns: Elements of Reusable Object-Oriented Software.* (Reading, Massachusetts: Addison-Wesley, 1994), pp. 325–330.

public behavior in a superclass by overriding virtual methods (see Rule 107):

```
class Object;

class LinkedList {
  public:
    void prepend(Object* object);
    const Object* first(void) const;
  protected:
    virtual void doPrepend(Object* object);
};

void
LinkedList::prepend(Object* object) {
  // Test precondition
  assert(object);

  doPrepend(object);

  // Test postcondition
  assert(first() == object);
}

class Stack : public LinkedList {
  protected:
    virtual void doPrepend(Object* object);
};
```

6.2 Class Design

60. *Keep Classes Simple*

If you are not sure that a method is required, do not add it. Do not add a method if other methods or a combination thereof can be used to efficiently provide the same functionality. It is much easier to add a method later than to take one out.

61. Define Subclasses So They May be Used Anywhere Their Superclasses May be Used

A subclass that changes or restricts the behavior of its parent class by overriding something is a *specialization* of that class, but its instances may have limited substitutability for the instances of its ancestor class. It may not always be possible to use the specialization anywhere the parent class could be used.

A subclass that is behaviorally compatible with a superclass is a *subtype* and its instances are fully substitutable for instances of its ancestor. A subclass that implements a subtype does not override the behavior of its ancestor class; it only extends the services provided by that class. A subtype has the same attributes and associations as its supertype.

The following design principles address the question of substitutability:

The Liskov Substitution Principle

> Methods that use references to superclasses must be able to use objects of subclasses without knowing it.[13]*

According to this principle, the ability to substitute a subclass object for a superclass object is characteristic of good design. Such designs offer more stability and reliability when compared with designs that fail to uphold this principle. When

---

[13] Barbara Liskov and John Guttag. *Abstraction and Specification in Program Development.* (New York: McGraw-Hill, 1986).

* This is our interpretation of Barbara Liskov's original formulation: "*If for each object O1 of type S there is an object O2 of type T such that for all programs P defined in terms of T, the behavior of P is unchanged when O1 is substituted for O2, then S is a subtype of T.*"

a design adheres to this principle, it generally indicates the designer did a good job identifying the base abstractions and generalizing their interfaces.

The Open-Closed Principle

> Software entities, i.e. classes, modules, functions, and so forth, should be open for extension, but closed for modification.[14,15]

Any design that requires code changes to handle the introduction of a newly derived class is a bad design. Whenever a subclass violates the existing contract between its superclasses and their clients, it forces changes in the existing code. When a method accepts a superclass instance, yet uses the derived type of this instance to control its behavior, changes are required for the introduction of each new subclass. Changes of this kind violate the *Open-Closed Principle* and are something to avoid.

Consider the following example:

```
class Shape {
  public:
    virtual resize(double scale) = 0;
};

class Rectangle : public Shape {
  public:
    void setWidth(double width);
    void setHeight(double height);
    double getWidth(void) const;
```

---

[14] Robert Martin. "Engineering Notebook: The Open-Closed Principle," C++ Report, Vol. 8, No. 1 (Jan 1996).
[15] Robert Martin. "Engineering Notebook," C++ Report, Vol. 8, No. 3 (Mar 1996).

```cpp
    double getHeight(void) const;
    void resize(double scale);
  private:
    double width_;
    double height_;
};

void Rectangle::resize(double scale) {
  setWidth(getWidth()*scale);
  setHeight(getHeight()*scale);
}
```

These classes form part of a simple hierarchy of shapes for a hypothetical drawing package. A Rectangle is described in terms of width and height. The resize() method is used to simultaneously change the width and height of a Rectangle.

Now suppose you decide that you want to add a new class to represent squares. A square is simply a specialized form of rectangle, so you create a class called Square that derives from Rectangle:

```cpp
class Square : public Rectangle {
  public:
    void setSize(double size);
    double getSize(void) const;
};
```

Since squares have identical width and height, you have added a setSize() method that always gives the width and height the same value:

```cpp
void Square::setSize(double size) {
    setWidth(size);
    setHeight(size);
}
```

However, this implementation has a problem; if a Square is passed as a Rectangle to another software entity that calls either setWidth() or setHeight() methods, the result might be a Square that no longer satisfies the width == height constraint. This behavior violates the *Liskov Substitution Principle*.

You might think to solve this problem by converting setWidth() and setHeight() into virtual methods and overriding those methods in Square to guarantee satisfaction of the constraint:

```cpp
class Rectangle : public Shape {
  public:
    // ...
    virtual void setWidth(double width);
    virtual void setHeight(double height);
    // ...
};

class Square : public Rectangle {
  public:
    // ...
    virtual void setWidth(double width);
    virtual void setHeight(double height);
    // ...
};

void Square::setWidth(double width) {
  Rectangle::setWidth(width);
  Rectangle::setHeight(width);
}

void Square::setHeight(double height) {
  Rectangle::setWidth(height);
  Rectangle::setHeight(height);
}
```

While this change solves the problem described above, it required modification of the `Rectangle` superclass, which you may or may not have the permission to change. Because this solution required changes in existing code, it violates the *Open-Closed Principle*. Not only that, but another problem still exists: if the `resize()` method, as implemented, is used to scale a `Rectangle` that is really a `Square`, the result again violates the `width == height` constraint:

```
Square square;
square.setSize(1);
square.resize(2);
// FAILS! Value is 4
assert(square.getWidth() == 2);
assert(square.getHeight() == 4);
```

The *Liskov Substitution* and *Open-Closed Principles* also apply to methods. In the following example, the `drawShape()` method in the `Canvas` class would have to be modified to handle a new shape class, such as `Square`:

```
class Canvas {
  public:
    void drawShape(const Shape& shape);
  protected:
    void drawCircle(const Circle& circle);
    void drawRectangle(const Rectangle& circle);
    // Add support for new shapes here...
};

void
Canvas::drawShape(const Shape& shape) {
  const Shape* pShape = &shape;
  // Use derived type to call relevant method
  if (typeid(*pShape) == typeid(Circle))
    drawCircle(
```

```
    *dynamic_cast<const Circle*>(pShape)
  );
  else if (typeid(*pShape) == typeid(Rectangle))
    drawRectangle(
      *dynamic_cast<const Rectangle*>(pShape)
    );
  // Add new shapes here ...
}
```

A developer would have to change the Canvas class and the drawShape() method each time they wanted to add a new subclass of the Shape class. Solve this problem by adding a drawSelf() method to the Shape subclasses and replacing the shape-specific methods on the canvas with a set of primitive drawing operations that Shape objects can use to draw themselves.[16] Each subclass of Shape would override the drawSelf() method to call the canvas drawing operations necessary to produce that particular shape:

```
class Canvas;

class Shape {
  public:
    virtual void drawSelf(Canvas* canvas) const
= 0;
};

class Circle : public Shape {
  public:
    virtual void drawSelf(Canvas* canvas) const;
};
```

---

[16] Also known as "double-dispatch." See Erich Gamma et al. *Design Patterns: Elements of Reusable Object-Oriented Software.* (Reading, Massachusetts, Addison-Wesley, 1994), pp. 338–339.

```
typedef std::list<Shape*> Shapes;

class Canvas {
  public:
    void drawShapes(const Shapes& shapes);
    // Define the operations the shapes will use
    void drawLine(int x1, int y1, int x2,
                  int y2);
    void drawCircle(int x, int y, int radius);
};

void
Canvas::drawShapes(const Shapes& shapes) {
  for (Shapes::const_iterator i=shapes.begin();
       i != shapes.end();
       i++) {
    (*i)->drawSelf(this);
  }
}
```

62. Use Inheritance for "is a" Relationships and Containment for "has a" Relationships

Making a choice between inheritance and containment is one of the most important decisions to be made in producing an object-oriented design. As a rule of thumb, use inheritance to model "is a" relationships, and containment to model "has a" relationships.

For example, a truck "*has a*" set of wheels and an ice-cream truck "*is a*" specialized kind of truck:

```
Class Wheel {
};

Class Truck {
```

```
  protected:
    vector<Wheel> wheels_;
};

Class IceCreamTruck : public Truck {
  // ...
};
```

63. *Avoid Multiple Inheritance*

Multiple inheritance adds significant complexity to design. With it, your design may be more difficult to understand, debug, and extend. While there are sometimes good reasons for using multiple inheritance, it is not a decision that you want to make casually. If you are tempted to use multiple inheritance, first consider whether your architecture might be simplified another way.

6.3 Thread Safety and Concurrency

Concurrency exists when two or more threads make progress, executing instructions at the same time. A single processor system can simulate concurrency by switching execution between two or more threads. A multiprocessor system can support parallel concurrency by executing a separate thread on each processor.

Many applications can benefit from the use of concurrency in their implementation. In a concurrent model of execution, an application is divided into two or more processes or threads, each executing in its own sequence of statements or instructions. An application may consist of one or more processes and a process may consist of one or more threads. Execution may be distributed among two or more machines in a network, two or more processors in a single machine, or interleaved on a single processor.

The separately executing processes or threads must generally compete for access to shared resources and data and must cooperate to accomplish their overall task.

Concurrent application development is a complicated task. Designing a concurrent application involves determining the necessary number of processes or threads, their particular responsibilities, and the methods by which they interact. It also involves determining the good, legal, or invariant program states and the bad or illegal program states. The critical problem is to find and implement a solution that maintains or guarantees good program states while prohibiting bad program states, even in those situations where two or more threads may be acting on the same resource.

In a concurrent environment, a programmer maintains desirable program states by limiting or negotiating access to shared resources using *synchronization*. The principal role of synchronization is to prevent undesirable or unanticipated interference between simultaneously executing instruction sequences.

Synchronization describes the set of mechanisms or processes for preventing undesirable interleaving of operations or interference between concurrent threads. This is primarily accomplished by serializing access to a shared program state. A programmer may choose between one of two synchronization techniques: *mutual exclusion* or *conditional synchronization*.

Mutual exclusion involves combining fine-grained atomic actions into coarse-grained actions and arranging to make these composite actions atomic.

Condition synchronization describes a process or mechanism that delays the execution of a thread until the program satisfies some predicate or condition.

A thread that is waiting on a synchronization mechanism is said to be *blocked*. Once a thread is *unblocked, awakened,* or *notified,* it is rescheduled for further execution.

Two basic uses exist for thread synchronization: to protect the integrity of shared data and to communicate changes in program state between cooperating threads.

An entity is *multithread-safe (MT-safe)* if multiple threads can simultaneously access that entity. Static class methods may support a different level of thread safety than those associated with an instance of that class. A class or method is considered *multithread-hot (MT-hot)* if it creates additional threads to accomplish its task.

The IEEE 1003.1 POSIX threads library defines a standard C language API for thread creation and synchronization. The Microsoft Windows™ API possesses a number of thread-related functions. Many C++ class libraries provide object-oriented wrappers for the functions provided by these APIs.

64. Design for Reentrancy

Always write code that is *reentrant,* that is, code that operates correctly when invoked recursively by a single thread or concurrently by multiple threads. To write reentrant code, do not use statically allocated resources, such as character buffers, unless you use some form of mutual exclusion to guarantee serialized access to that resource. Examples of static resources include shared objects, shared memory, I/O devices, and other hardware resources.

65. Use Threads only Where Appropriate

Multithreading does not equate to improved application performance. Some applications are not suited for multithreading and may run slower following the introduction of multiple threads because of the overhead required to manage those threads.

Before you multithread your application, determine whether it can benefit from their use. Use threads if your application needs[17]

- To simultaneously respond to many events, e.g., a web browser or server.
- To provide a high level of responsiveness, e.g., a user interface implementation that can continue to respond to user actions even while the application is performing other computations.
- To take advantage of machines with multiple processors.

66. Avoid Unnecessary Synchronization

Synchronization can be expensive. On many platforms, the operating system kernel manages interthread synchronization and signaling. On such systems, operations that affect thread scheduling require a context switch to the kernel, which is expensive.

Synchronization serializes access to an object thereby minimizing potential concurrency. Before synchronizing code, consider whether that code accesses shared state information. If a method only operates on independently synchronized objects, local variables, or non-volatile data members, such as those initialized during construction, then synchronization is not required.

Do not synchronize fundamental data types or structures, such as lists, vectors, etc. Let the users of these objects determine whether external synchronization is necessary.

---

[17] Doug Lea. *Concurrent Programming in Java*™: *Design Principles and Patterns.* (Reading, Massachusetts: Addison-Wesley, 1997), pp. 1–2.

67. *Do Not Synchronize Access to Code That Does Not Change Shared State*

To maximize concurrency in a program, you must minimize the frequency and duration of lock acquisition. When you use a mutual exclusion lock to define a *critical section*—a sequence of statements that you want to execute in an atomic fashion—you serialize access to all of the code contained in that critical section. If you include statements that do not modify shared state within a critical section, you increase the amount of time that other threads must wait before they may enter that critical section. This might reduce the maximum concurrency that could be achieved by your application.

7.

Programming
Conventions

This chapter describes recommended C++ programming conventions.

7.1 Preprocessor

68. Use '#include"..."' for Collocated Header Files and '#include<...>' for External Header Files

While not specified by the C or C++ standards, most compilers first search the directory of the file that contains the #include when you use the quoted form.

You can take advantage of this behavior to distinguish between header files that are part of the public interface and those that are not. Use the bracket form of #include for external header files and the quoted form for files that are collocated with the including file:

```cpp
// MyClass.cpp

#include "MyClass.h"
#include <vector>
#include <sys/types.h>
// ...
```

69. Place Preprocessor Include Guards in Header Files

Use preprocessor guards to prevent the duplicate declarations that would result should the contents of a header file be included multiple times. Place these guards in the header files, not in the files with the #include.

The following implementation is incorrect:

```
— MyClass.h
#define MyClass_h
// ...

— A file that uses MyClass.h
#ifndef MYCLASS_H // Bad!
#include "MyClass.h"
#endif // MYCLASS_H
```

The following implementation is correct:

```
— MyClass.h
#ifndef MYCLASS_H // Good!
#define MyClass_h
// ...
#endif // MYCLASS_H

— A file that uses MyClass.h
#include "MyClass.h" // Good!
```

70. Use #if..#endif and #ifdef..#endif Instead of "/* ... */" Comments to Hide Blocks of Code

Use the preprocessor directives, #if and #ifdef, to hide deprecated, unfinished, temporary, test, or obsolete code. Using /* ... */ comment blocks may lead to syntax errors if the code already contains comment blocks.

Library developers often retain deprecated code for one or more library releases to give their users some time to update their code. Wrap deprecated code with an #if...#endif pair to provide a mechanism that users of your library can use to disable deprecated code when they are ready to update those sections of their code that rely on the deprecated features.

```cpp
class MyClass {
  public:
    #ifdef DEPRECATED
      void method(void);
    #endif
    void method(size_t start, size_t end);
};

void
MyClass::method(size_t start, size_t end) {
  #ifdef ECHO_CHECK
    std::cout << static_cast<int>(start);
    std::cout << ",";
    std::cout << static_cast<int>(end);
    std::cout << std::endl;
  #endif

  #if TBD // {
  anotherMethod(start,end);
  #endif  // }

  // ...

  #if TBD
  yetAnotherMethod(void);
  #endif
}
```

You may want to mark your directives with end-of-line comments that contain block delimiter characters such as " [" and "] ". These characters can be used to locate the beginning and end of the block in editors that provide matching brace navigation.

71. Use Macros Sparingly

Bjarne Stroustrup writes:

> "The first rule about macros is: Do not use them if you do not have to. Almost every macro demonstrates a flaw in the programming language, in the program, or in the programmer."[18]

Instead of macros, prefer constants, enumerations, inline functions, or templates. The primary practical uses for macros in C++ are conditional compilation and special cases where you need compilation unit filenames and line numbers (see Rule 73). To see how you can use templates to replace parameterized macros, see Rule 116. See also Rules 78 and 88.

See also Chapter 18 of Stroustrup's *The Design and Evolution of C++*[19] for an interesting (non-complimentary) perspective on the preprocessor.

72. Add a Semicolon after Every Statement Expression Macro

Add a semicolon after every macro that expands into one or more statements. Without a trailing semicolon, the code may not compile, and the auto-indentation function provided by many editors may become confused:

---

[18] Bjarne Stroustrup. *The C++ Programming Language, Third Edition.* (Reading, Massachusetts: Addison-Wesley, 1997), p. 160.
[19] Bjarne Stroustrup. *The Design and Evolution of C++.* (Reading, Massachusetts: Addison-Wesley, 1994), section 11.7.

```cpp
void foo() {
  TRACE_BEGIN            // Bad
  MACRO_FUNCTION(foo)    // Bad
  // ...
}

void bar() {
  TRACE_BEGIN;           // Good!
  MACRO_FUNCTION(bar);   // Good!
  // ...
}
```

73. Use Macros to Capture the Current File Name and Line Number

Most of the time, you should use inline or template functions for inline code expansion. However, you must use a macro if you want to capture the file name and line number at the expansion point:

```cpp
template <typename ReturnType,
          typename Arg0Type,
          typename Val0Type>
ReturnType traceCall(ReturnType
                     (*function)(Arg0Type),
                     Val0Type arg0,
                     const char* file,
                     int line) {
  // Do Trace ...
  std::cout << file << ":" << line << std::endl;
  return (*function)(arg0);
}

// Use macro to capture the file name and
// line number
```

```
#define TRACE_CALL_1ARG(function,arg0) \
    traceCall(function, arg0, __FILE__,__LINE__);

void foo(const char* message);
int bar(const char* message);

void doSomething() {
  TRACE_CALL_1ARG(foo,"Message");
  int result =TRACE_CALL_1ARG(bar,"Message");
}
```

74. *Do Not Use "*#define*" to Define Constants—Declare* static const *Variables Instead*

A "#define" is expanded by the preprocessor while constants are processed by the compiler and are included in the symbolic information used to debug the code:

```
#define PI 3.14159               // Bad
static const double Pi = 3.14159;  // Good!
```

7.2 Declarations

75. *Use Portable Types for Portable Code*

The C++ Standard specifies a number of language features as "implementation defined." The vendors of C++ compilers were given the freedom to choose their implementation for these features. This unfortunate situation has created a number of portability issues for anyone who is trying to create a cross-platform C++ product.

The most common portability issue revolves around the sizes of the intrinsic numeric types. While the standard guarantees certain ordering between the types, the actual bit-length of each type largely depends on choices made by the compiler vendor and the hardware for which the compiler generates code. This is becoming more of an issue with the introduction of 64-bit processors. Even the sign of the char type is implementation defined.

If your code depends on the size, range, or precision of the numeric types, then you likely need to use or define a system of non-standard types that have known bit-sizes.

Most Linux and Unix platforms provide an include file called "inttypes.h" that defines a number of platform-independent numeric types, such as uint8, or int32. The inttypes.h file defines these new types using typedef declarations based on the existing numerical types.

Many projects create portable type definitions using tools that dynamically characterize the programming environment. These tools test for the existence of certain optional types, and determine the size of each.

If you want to write portable code, and your code makes certain assumptions about the existence, size, or sign of built-in types, then you should consider using these portable types instead of the built-in types.

76. Use Typedefs to Simplify Complicated Type Expressions

Repeated use of complex type expressions makes your code more difficult to read and comprehend—the reader has to expend greater effort to determine whether two expressions refer to the same type:

```
class Bad {
  public:
    void setCallback(
      int (*callback)(int, const char*)
    );
```

```
    void addToLog(
      const vector<pair<Date,const char*> >& log
    );
    const vector<const char*>& getLog() const;
  private:
    int (*callback_)(int, const char*);
    std::vector<std::pair<Date,const char*> >
log_;
};
```

Use a typedef to replace each complicated type expression
with a single type name to reduce the visual complexity of
your code and to ease the reader's task of reconciling multiple
uses of the same type:

```
class Good {
  public:
    typedef int (*Callback)(int,const char*);
// Good!
    typedef pair<Date,const char*> LogEntry;
// Good!
    typedef const vector<LogEntry> Log; // Good!

    void setCallback(Callback callback);
    void addToLog(const Log& log);
    const Log& getLog() const;
  private:
    Callback callback_;
    Log log_;
};
```

77. Create a Zero-Valued Enumerator to Indicate an Uninitialized, Invalid, Unspecified, or Default State

Define an enumerator with a name such as "None,"
"Unspecified," "Unknown," or "Invalid," to provide

a type-safe means for testing the validity of an enumeration variable:

```
enum Color {
  None,
  Red,
  Green,
  Blue
};
```

Make this enumerator the first one in the enumeration. By doing so, you reduce the chance that this enumerator would get overlooked if others add new enumerators to the list, and you also allow the compiler to automatically give the enumerator a value of zero, making it easy to catch an invalid value using a runtime assertion.

You may also use the first enumerator to define a default value:

```
enum Color {
  Default,
  Red,
  Green,
  Blue = Default
};
```

78. *Do Not Define Enumerations Using Macros or Integer Constants*

Developers experienced in languages without enumerated types might be tempted to write something like this:

```
#define COLOR_RED        1
#define COLOR_BLUE       2
#define COLOR_GREEN      3
int defaultColor = COLOR_RED;
```

or,

```
static const int ColorRed = 1;
static const int ColorBlue = 2;
static const int ColorGreen = 3;

int defaultColor = ColorRed;
```

This approach sacrifices a considerable amount of type safety, creating the disastrous possibility that the compiler would cheerfully accept

```
int defaultColor = DEGREES_CELSIUS;
```

In C++ an enumeration is a separate type,[20] so using them allows the compiler to enforce a certain amount of type safety. If type safety is not a compelling enough reason, perhaps a practical one is that an `enum` value is much more likely to be displayed in symbolic form in a debugger, whereas a `#define` is likely displayed as a numeric value.

See also Rules 82 and 86.

7.3 Scoping

79. Declare Enumerations within a Namespace or Class

To avoid symbolic name conflicts between enumerators and other global names, nest `enum` declarations within the most closely related class or common namespace. If this is not possible, prefix each enumerator name with a unique identifier such as the enumeration or module name.

---

[20] Bjarne Stroustrup, *The Design and Evolution of C++*. (Reading, Massachusetts: Addison-Wesley, 1994), chapter 18.

80. Declare Global Functions, Variables, or Constants as Static Members of a Class

If a global variable or constant closely relates to one class more than any other, make that variable or constant a member of that class.

If you have constants that relate to a specific topic or field of study, use an appropriately named class to group those constants; for example, use a class named Math to hold constants for values such as *pi*, *e*, etc.

Prefer classes over namespaces when scoping static variables and constants. Each class should have its own source file in which you can place the initialization statements for these static class members. Namespaces are not typically assigned independent source files.

81. Declare for-loop Iteration Variables Inside of for Statements

Iteration variables should be declared inside a for statement. This limits the scope of the variable to the for statement:

```
for (size_t count = 0; count < length; count++)
{
  // count is only visible inside this block...
}
```

7.4 Functions and Methods

82. Use an Enumeration Instead of a Boolean to Improve Readability

The meaning of a Boolean function parameter is often lost when a developer encounters an invocation of that function. Replacing a Boolean parameter with an enumeration can

improve the readability of the code and relieves the viewer of
the need to review documentation just to discover the meaning
of the argument:

```cpp
class Caller {
  public:
    typedef void (*Callback)();
    enum Duration {
      DeleteAfterCall,
      KeepAfterCall
    };
void addCallback(Callback callback,
                 bool keepAfter);
void addCallback(Callback callback,
                 Duration duration);
};


void
callback() {
  // ...
}


void
doSomething() {
  Caller caller;

  // But what did 'true' mean?
  caller.addCallback(callback,true);

  // The choice of behavior is obvious in
  // this call...
  caller.addCallback(callback,
                     Caller::KeepAfterCall);
}
```

83. *Use an Object Pointer Instead of a Reference if a Function Stores a Reference or Pointer to the Object*

A non-const reference parameter indicates that your function may perform non-const operations on the object but does not indicate whether that function saves a reference to the object. Use a pointer instead of a reference to indicate that your function stores a reference or pointer to the object passed as an argument.

In the following example it is not immediately obvious that a reference to each element is stored—the use of a non-const reference simply indicates that the elements might be modified:

```
class ListElement {
  public:
    ListElement(ListElement& prev,
                ListElement& next);
  private:
    ListElement* prev_;
    ListElement* next_;
};

ListElement::ListElement(ListElement& prev,
                         ListElement& next)
  : prev_(&prev), next_(&next) {
}
```

When you use pointers, you give a hint that a reference to an object might be stored:

```
class ListElement {
  public:
    ListElement(ListElement* prev,
                ListElement* next);
  private:
    ListElement* prev_;
```

```
    ListElement* next_;
};

ListElement::ListElement(ListElement* prev,
                         ListElement* next)
  : prev_(prev), next_(next) {
}
```

84. *Accept Objects by Reference and Primitive or Pointer Types by Value*

In general, functions that modify arguments passed by reference can hamper program readability. However, to improve performance of argument passing and to avoid unnecessary copy construction, pass objects and structures (particularly large ones) by reference. If the passed object is not modified within the function, declare it as const to enforce its integrity:

```
void importantFunction(const BigObject& param);
```

However, do not declare primitive types, such as char, int, or pointers, as reference parameters, since these types are often most efficiently passed by value.

85. *Use a* const char* *for Narrow Character String Parameters*

Use const char* instead of string class instances for functions that do not modify the string. Use a string class to store a copy of a const char* argument internally.

A const char* parameter provides greater flexibility because it can be used with almost any C++ string class implementation since most string implementations provide methods that return a const char* pointer to the string contents. If you use a string class in the interface, you may force your users to copy string contents from one string object to another string of a different type.

86. *Pass Enumerator Values, Not Integer Constants*

Use an enum statement to identify the integral ordinal values that describe a specific concept or property, e.g., color, direction, type, mode, etc. Enumerations provide a level of type safety that simple integer constants cannot—integer values must be validated with runtime tests to ensure that they represent a legal value—enumerations normally do not.

However, do not use enumerations for bit mask values because you need to cast enumerator values to integers prior to performing bit-level operations. Use regular integer constants and variables for bit-level operations.

See also Rules 78 and 82.

87. *Do Not Use* void* *in a Public Interface*

Because any pointer can be cast to a void* pointer type, a void* pointer bypasses the normal type-checking used to provide type safety in the C++ language. You may choose to use void* pointers within your private implementation, but you should always present a type-safe external interface to the users of your software.

You will not likely be able to avoid all use of void* pointers, because these form an integral part of many standard C libraries.

You should never use void* in a public C++ interface. There are many situations where you might use void* pointers to create reusable software components, but these should always be wrapped with templates to provide a typed interface. Many pointer collection classes can be refactored into a superclass that manipulates void* pointers, and which is then wrapped with a template class or derived from to provide a type-safe interface for that collection. This approach is often used with template collections to reduce the amount of code generated by different instantiations of the same template.

88. *Use Inline Functions Instead of Macros*

When possible, use inline functions instead of macros. Inline functions provide typed parameters without the overhead of a function call, while macros are simply textual replacements.

89. *Inline Only the Simplest of Functions*

Inline functions should be as short as possible—usually not more than three or four lines. Be aware that using the `inline` qualifier is just a hint to the compiler, one that the compiler is not required to heed.

90. *Factor Functions to Allow Inlining of Trivial Cases*

If you can divide the implementation of a method into trivial and non-trivial cases, consider factoring the method into a single inline function that implements the trivial case(s) and calls one or more out-of-line methods that implement the more complex cases. This gives the compiler the opportunity to inline the code used in the trivial cases:

```
class Foo {
  public:
    inline void doSomething(void);
  protected:
    void doSomethingComplicated(void);
  private:
    enum State {
      Simple,
      Complicated
    } state_;
};

inline void
Foo::doSomething(void) {
  if (state_ == Simple) {
    // Inline the code for trivial case here ...
  }
```

```
  else {
    // Call a non-inline function for
    // complicated case...
    doSomethingComplicated();
  }
}
```

7.5 Classes

91. Define Small Classes and Small Methods

Smaller classes and methods are easier to design, code, test, document, read, understand, and use. Because smaller classes generally have fewer methods and represent simpler concepts, their interfaces tend to exhibit better cohesion.

Try to limit the interface of each class to the bare minimum number of methods required to provide the necessary functionality. Avoid the temptation to add "convenience" forms of a method when only one general-purpose form suffices.

All sorts of informal guidelines exist for establishing the maximum size of a class or method—use your best judgment. If a class or method seems too big, then consider refactoring that class or method into additional classes or methods. Do not hesitate to factor a large method into smaller, private methods even if you only call these smaller methods once from within another method. The subdivided code will be easier to understand, and you might yet discover that you can reuse some of the new methods.

92. Build Fundamental Classes from Standard Types

When designing low-level fundamental or concrete types, you should strive to minimize dependencies on non-native, non-standard types. Every time you include a non-standard type in the interface of a fundamental type, you introduce a new and potentially volatile dependency. Such dependencies may not only make your code more susceptible to change, but also increases the compilation and execution "footprint" of that code.

Limit yourself to the types defined by the C++ language and the C++ Standard Library whenever possible.

93. Avoid the Use of Virtual Base Classes in User-Extensible Class Hierarchies

A user that extends a class hierarchy that possesses virtual base classes may not be aware that they may need to invoke a virtual superclass constructor in the constructors of their subclass. If you expect users to extend a class that has a virtual base class, you need to fully describe if and how they must initialize the superclass, perhaps forcing you to reveal implementation details that might have best remained hidden.

If you must use virtual superclasses, try to design your implementation such that the virtual superclass can be initialized using a default constructor—the compiler automatically invokes this constructor if the user fails to specify a superclass initializer in the constructor of their instantiable class.

94. Declare the Access Level of All Members

Do not assume that others will remember the default access level of a class [private] or struct [public]. When possible, group declarations into a single section for each access level. Many programmers declare sections in the following order: public, followed by protected, followed by private.

95. Declare All Member Variables Private

Prefer private over protected access for class data members. Declare all data members private and use "accessor" functions to give subclasses access to those private data members. This is especially true for classes that you provide as superclasses

for end users to extend by subclassing. Always treat the implementation details as private information to reduce the impact
on dependent classes should the implementation change.

The following code gives the subclass direct access to the superclass data member:

```cpp
class Superclass {
  protected:
    Foo foo_; // Currently referenced by value
};

class Subclass : public Superclass {
  public:
    void method(void);
};

void
Subclass::method(void) {
  foo_.fooMethod(); // Incorrect!
}
```

The type and existence of the foo_ member may depend
entirely on the implementation chosen. Make the member
private and use a protected or public method to provide access
to the abstract representation:

```cpp
class Superclass {
  protected:
    Foo& getFoo(void);
  private:   // Right!
    Foo foo_;
};

Foo*
Superclass::getFoo(void) {
```

```
    return &foo_;
}

class Subclass : public Superclass {
  public:
    void method(void);
};

void Subclass::method(void) {
  getFoo()->fooMethod();
}
```

96. *Avoid the Use of Friend Declarations*

Friend declarations are often indicative of poor design because they bypass access restrictions and hide dependencies between classes and functions. You should only use them when you want to prevent a subclass from gaining access to certain superclass methods while allowing certain helper classes, global operators, and functions to access those same methods.

A common misuse of friend declarations is to grant global operators access to the private or protected members of the operand classes. In many cases, the operations performed can be accomplished using normal public member functions. For example, global Boolean comparison operators can often be implemented by calling an equivalent comparison function on the operand class:

```
class A {
  public:
    int compareTo(const A& other) const;
};

bool operator==(const A& lhs, const A&rhs) {
  return lhs.compareTo(rhs)==0; // Good!
}
```

One scenario where a friend declaration might be required is in the implementation of *handle-body* pattern.[21] The base body class must often give the corresponding handle class access to the reference counting and other lifecycle methods of the body without giving subclasses access to these same members.

7.6 Class Members

97. Declare an Explicit Default Constructor for Added Clarity

Declare a default constructor for every class you create. Although some compilers may be able to automatically generate a more efficient implementation in some situations, choose an explicit default constructor for added clarity.

You should declare and implement a public default constructor to make it clear that your class supports default construction. You should define one even if there are no initializers and the function body is empty. If you allow the compiler to generate the constructor, you may fail to consider all of the initialization requirements for your class. When you supply a default constructor you provide source code that can be used for setting debug breakpoints and execution tracing.

You should declare a protected default constructor if your class does not support default construction. Directly instantiating a default instance would produce a compilation error. You only need to provide an implementation for a protected constructor if you want to provide default construction functionality to subclasses (see also Rule 100).

You should declare a private default constructor if your class does not support default construction or consists only of static

---

[21] Erich Gamma et al. *Design Patterns: Elements of Reusable Object-Oriented Software*. (Reading, Massachusetts: Addison-Wesley, 1994), p. 155.

members. Directly instantiating a default instance would produce a compilation error. You do not need to provide an implementation in this case since the constructor will never be invoked (unless you claim an exception to Rule 96 and decide to use friends; see also Rule 101).

Note also that if you provide any other constructors, the compiler generally does not generate a default constructor for you.

98. *Always Declare a Copy Constructor, Assignment Operator, and Destructor if the Class can be Instantiated*

Although the compiler provides these automatically, there are benefits to hand-coding them. An explicit implementation forces you to consciously decide on the semantics of copying and the cleanup of your objects. It is easier to change your code by having these functions implemented and documented. Though for very simple classes it might not be necessary to define them, define them all if you define any.

You should declare a protected or private copy constructor and assignment operator if your class does not support copy construction or assignment (see Rules 100 and 101).

A similar access restriction strategy exists for virtual destructors (see Rule 102).

99. *Always Implement a Virtual Destructor If Your Class May be Subclassed*

Declare a destructor `virtual` to properly destroy derived objects through base pointers.

Given the following,

```
class Base {
  public:
    Base(void);
    ~Base();                    // Bad
};
```

```cpp
class Derived : public Base {
  public:
    Derived(void);
    ~Derived();                    // Bad
};

Derived::Derived(void) {
  // allocate a resource
}

Derived::~Derived() {
  // free that resource
}

void cleanup(Base* b) {
  delete b;
}
```

if cleanup() is passed a pointer to an instance of Derived, the delete expression invokes the Base class destructor but not the Derived destructor. If you declare the Base destructor to be virtual, then the delete operation calls the Derived destructor and any allocated resources are freed:

```cpp
class Base {
  public:
    Base(void);
    virtual ~Base();              // Good
};

class Derived : public Base {
  public:
    Derived(void);
    virtual ~Derived();           // Good
};
```

100. Make Constructors Protected to Prohibit Direct Instantiation

To prohibit direct instantiation of an abstract class, you should only allow protected access to all of its constructors. Derived classes will still be able to construct the abstract class, but other entities will not.

You also need to declare a protected default constructor and copy constructor even if they are not going to be used. Derived classes can still use the protected copy constructor from within their own copy constructors if desired.

101. Make Constructors Private to Prohibit Derivation

To prohibit derivation from a "closed" class, declare all constructors as private. Use a public static method to instantiate the class. This method acts as a "factory" for the class.[22] You also need to declare a private default constructor and copy constructor even if they are not going to be used:

```
#include <memory>

class ClosedClass {
  public:
    // Use this function to construct an
    // instance.
    static
    std::auto_ptr<ClosedClass> makeClosedClass();
  private:
    ClosedClass(void);
    ClosedClass(const ClosedClass& other);
};
```

---

[22] Erich Gamma et al. *Design Patterns: Elements of Reusable Object-Oriented Software.* (Reading, Massachusetts: Addison-Wesley, 1994), pp. 107–116.

```
ClosedClass::ClosedClass(void) {
  // ...
}

std::auto_ptr<ClosedClass>
ClosedClass::makeClosedClass(void) {
  return std::auto_ptr<ClosedClass>
            (new ClosedClass());
}

// Illegal! This derivation cannot be
// instantiated!
class Derived : public ClosedClass {
  public:
// No access to ClosedClass constructors!
Derived(void);
};
```

102. *Declare a Private* operator new() *to Prohibit Dynamic Allocation*

When you give a class a private operator new(), you prevent users from being able to allocate instances of that class using the new keyword. This occurs because the compiler cannot grant access to the private implementation of new.

Use this technique when implementing classes that provide "Resource Acquisition is Initialization" (RAII) based resource management. The RAII technique relies on the construction and destruction of automatically allocated objects to peform resource acquisition and release—the constructor of an RAII object acquires a resource and the destructor releases it. This behavior provides some degree of exception safety (see Rule 156).

Implementation of RAII relies on automatic allocation of objects—the benefits provided by RAII objects are lost if these objects are dynamically allocated on the heap.

If you simply add a declaration for a private operator new() to your class, you can disallow dynamic allocation for that class:

```
class Mutex {
  public:
    Mutex(void);
    void acquire(void);
    void release(void);
    class Lock {
      public:
        Lock(Mutex& mutex);
        ~Lock();
      private:
        // Prohibit dynamic allocation
        // Note: No implementation is required!
        void* operator new (size_t);
        void* operator new[] (size_t);
        Mutex& mutex_;
    };
};

Mutex::Lock::Lock(Mutex& mutex)
  : mutex_(mutex) {
  mutex_.acquire();
}

Mutex::Lock::~Lock() {
  mutex_.release();
}
```

```
class A {
  public:
    void bad(void);
    void good(void);
  private:
    Mutex mutex_;
};


void A::bad() {
  // If you define a private operator new(), the
  // following will produce a compile-time
  // error!
  Mutex::Lock* lock = new Mutex::Lock(mutex_);
  // ...
  if (error) throw std::exception();
  // ...
  delete lock; // Bad! Throw will skip this!
}


void A::good() {
  Mutex::Lock lock(mutex_); // Good!
  // ...
  if (error) throw std::exception();
  // ...
  // lock is always destroyed and mutex
  // released
}
```

103. Declare a Protected or Private Destructor to Prohibit Static or Automatic Allocation

Situations sometimes arise where you want to disallow static or automatic allocation of objects—you want create a class that only supports heap allocation using new().

You can accomplish this by giving your class a private or protected destructor. A compiler does not allow you to create a
static or automatic instance of a class that does not have a
public destructor:

```
#include <memory>

class HeapOnly {
public:
  HeapOnly(void);
private:
  // Give auto_ptr<> access to destructor
friend class std::auto_ptr<HeapOnly>;
  // Prohibit static or automatic allocation
  ~HeapOnly(); // Dynamic allocation only
};

HeapOnly s; // Oops! compilation error

std::auto_ptr<HeapOnly> p(new HeapOnly()); // OK
```

Under what circumstances would you use this technique?
Consider a handle-body implementation[23] that controls the
life span of body instances by counting references. Each body
maintains a count of the handles that reference it. When the
user destroys the last handle reference, the reference count is
decremented to zero, and the body deletes itself by calling
delete.

Since this implementation uses a count of handle references to
govern the destruction of a body object, the user must not destroy the body object while any handle objects still refer to it.

---

[23] Erich Gamma et al. *Design Patterns: Elements of Reusable Object-Oriented Software*. (Reading, Massachusetts: Addison-Wesley, 1994), p. 155.

This implies that you cannot allow users to construct automatic body objects, because they would be destroyed at scope exit while handle references may continue to exist outside of that scope.

In addition, the implementation cannot use `delete` to destroy an object that the user allocated in static or automatic storage. To eliminate this possibility, the implementation defines a protected destructor for the body class:

```
class Handle; // Forward reference

class Body { // Base class for body classes
  friend class Handle;
  public:
    Body(void);
  protected:
    virtual ~Body();
  private:
    void addReference(void);
    void removeReference(void);
    size_t count_;
};

Body::Body()
 : count_(0) {
}

Body::~Body() {
}

void
Body::addReference(void) {
  ++count_;
}
```

```
void
Body::removeReference(void) {
  if (0 == --count_) delete this;
}
```

The Handle class implementation updates the reference count of the assigned Body objects:

```
class Handle {
  public:
    Handle(Body* body);
    Handle(const Handle& other);
    Handle& operator=(const Handle& other);
    ~Handle();
  private:
    Body* body_;
};


Handle::Handle(Body* body)
  : body_(body) {
  body_->addReference();
}


Handle::Handle(const Handle& handle)
  : body_(handle.body_) {
  body_->addReference();
}


Handle& Handle::operator=(const Handle& other) {
  Body* temp = body_;
  other.body_->addReference();
  body_ = other.body_;
  temp->removeReference();
```

```
return *this;
}

Handle::~Handle() {
  body_->removeReference();
}

// Body b;                     // Not allowed!

Handle first(new Body());    // OK!
Handle second(first);        // Makes a copy
```

104. Declare Single-Parameter Constructors as explicit to Avoid Unexpected Type Conversions

A compiler can use a single parameter constructor for type conversions. While this is natural in some situations, it might be unexpected in others. Consider the following declaration:

```
MyClass c = 42;
```

If MyClass does not possess an assignment operator to handle this case, the compiler tries to initialize c with a constructor MyClass(42). See Stroustrup for a discussion of the potential pitfalls associated with implicit conversions.[24]

You can avoid this behavior by declaring a constructor with the explicit keyword, e.g.,

```
class MyClass {
  public:
    explicit MyClass(int n);
};
```

---

[24] Bjarne Stroustrup, *The C++ Programming Language, Third Edition.* (Reading, Massachusetts: Addison-Wesley, 1997), section 11.7.1.

105. *Use Default Arguments to Reduce the Number of Constructors*

The need to provide multiple options for classes can easily lead to many different constructors. For example, you might find a class like this:

```
class Brush {
  public:
    Brush(void);                 // default brush
    Brush(Color c);              // color
    Brush(Color c, Texture t);   // color, texture
};
```

It is likely that the implementations of these constructors are substantially similar. If so, use default arguments to reduce redundancy:

```
Brush(Color c = Color.Black;
      Texture t = Texture.Solid);
```

With this single constructor, a Brush object can be constructed with no parameters, just a Color parameter, or both Color and Texture parameters.

106. *Do Not Overload Non-Virtual Methods in Subclasses*

Do not use a method name in a subclass if a method of that name already exists in an ancestor class, unless that method is a virtual method.[25]

```
#include <iostream>

class B {
```

---

[25] Tom Cargill. "C++ Gotchas: Tutorial Notes." p. 13. Distributed at these seminars: http://www.profcon.com/profcon/Gotchas.htm.

```
  public:
    void foo(double d);
};

void
B::foo(double d) {
  std::cout << "B::foo(" << d << ")";
  std::cout << std::endl;
}

class D : public B {
  public:
    void foo(int i);
};

void
D::foo (int i) {
  std::cout << "D::foo(" << i << ")";
  std::cout << std::endl;
}

int main() {
  D d;
  d.foo(1.5);
  return 0;
}
```

which results in the following output:

```
D::foo(1)
```

If a client wanted to call the inherited version of foo(), it could be done with the line

```
d.B::foo(1.5);
```

Note that foo() is NOT virtual. If it had been virtual, the compiler would have warned about hiding the inherited version of foo().

107. Declare Virtual Methods Protected and Call Them from Public Non-Virtual Methods

Do not expose virtual methods in the public interface of a class. Use a public method with a similar name to call the protected virtual method.

You should view polymorphism via virtual methods as a contract between a superclass and potential subclasses, the details of which should remain in the protected interface of each class.

The designer of a superclass can use the public method to ensure that certain operations, such as pre- and postcondition tests (see Rule 152), execution tracing, and serialization, are performed even when a subclass overrides the virtual function:

```
class Superclass {
  public:
    void update(void);
  protected:
    virtual void doUpdate(void);
  private:
    // Used with Lock for serialization
    Mutex mutex_;
};
void Superclass::update() {
  // Generated for subclasses too.
  trace("update()");
  // Serialized for subclasses too.
  Lock lock(mutex_);
  doUpdate();
}
```

```cpp
class Subclass : public Superclass {
  protected:
    virtual void doUpdate(void);
};
```

108. Keep Your Functions "const-correct"

If a class method does not modify any member variables, declare it const.

If a function does not modify an argument, make the parameter type const. (Of course, modification of the argument cannot occur when it is passed by value.)

If you do not want to allow a caller to modify the object referenced by a function return value, or if you want to force the caller to construct a copy of the referenced object, declare the return reference type as const.

109. Use Object Pointers and References in Class Declarations

Use pointers and references to avoid introducing a compile-time dependency on a complete class declaration when a simple forward declaration would suffice. This approach has two benefits: you can use it to eliminate circular dependencies and you can reduce the number of header files that the compiler must process.

```cpp
— Foo.h
#include "Bar.h" // Complete declaration of
class B

class Foo {
  public:
    // Requires complete declaration of B
    Foo(Bar b);
```

```
  private:
    // Requires complete declaration of B
    Bar b_;
};
```

— Foo.h (Better)

```
// Forward declaration instead of #include
class Bar;
class Foo {
  public:
    // Forward declaration will suffice.
    Foo(const Bar& b);
  private:
    // Forward declaration will suffice.
    Bar* bp_;
};
```

— Foo.cpp

```
#include <Foo.h>
// Source gets complete declaration.
#include <Bar.h>
```

7.7 Operators

110. *Adhere to the Natural Semantics of Operators*

Do not define operator overloads unless the results are intuitive to someone unfamiliar with the code. Do provide operator overloads when it is more natural to express logic using standard mathematical operators. For example, it makes intuitive sense to provide operator+()for a currency class; but it probably does not make intuitive sense to provide that operator for a customer class.

111. Do Not Overload `operator&&()` *or* `operator||()`[26]

C++ uses *short-circuit evaluation* for Boolean expressions. This means that evaluation of a Boolean expression proceeds from left to right and stops once the overall truth or falseness of an expression has been determined—any additional subexpressions are not evaluated beyond this point. Most programmers expect and rely on short-circuit evaluation in their programs. For example, consider the ubiquitous Boolean expression that checks to make sure a pointer is not zero prior to its use:

```
char* str;
// Check for non empty string
if ((str != 0) || str[0] != '\0') {
  // ...
}
```

If you overload `operator&&()` or `operator||()` you replace short-circuit evaluation semantics with that of function call semantics. If you overload the `operator&&()` member function, then what you see as

```
if (expression1 && expression2)   // ...
```

the compiler interprets as

```
if (expression1.operator&&(expression2)) // ...
```

If you overload the global `operator&&()` function, the compiler interprets that same expression as

```
if (operator&&(expression1, expression2)) // ...
```

The difference between the function call semantics and short-circuit semantics is that all of the arguments must

---

[26] Scott Meyers. *More Effective C++*. (Reading, Massachusetts: Addison-Wesley, 1996), pp. 35–38.

be evaluated—in this case, the result cannot be determined until expression1 and expression2 are evaluated and the operator&&() method is executed. To complicate matters, the C++ Standard does not specify the order of evaluation for function arguments so you do not know which expression the compiler evaluates first.

To avoid surprising your users with unexpected behavior do not overload these operators. If you want to be able to use instances of a class in a Boolean expression, consider implementing a bool or int conversion operator instead (but not both):

```
class Result {
  public:
    operator bool() const;   // do this
    // operator int() const; // or this
};

void f(const Result& r1, const Result& r2) {
  if (r1 && r2) {
    // ...
  }
}
```

112. Invoke the Superclass Assignment Operator(s) in the Assignment Operator of a Subclass

You should not replicate operations normally performed by a superclass assignment operator within a subclass—your subclass would require knowledge of the implementation of that parent class. If the implementation of a superclass assignment operator changes you may have to change the assignment operator in your subclass. To simplify your assignment operators and to insulate your class from changes in a superclass, you should always call the superclass assignment operator to allow it to perform whatever operations are required:

```
class Base {
  public:
    Base& operator=(const Base& other);
  private:
    int foo_;
};

Base&
Base::operator=(const Base& that) {
  foo_ = that.foo_;
  return *this;
}

class Derived : public Base {
  public:
    Derived& operator=(const Derived& that);
  private:
    int bar_;
};

Derived&
Derived::operator=(const Derived& that) {
  Base::operator=(that);
  bar_ = that.bar_;
  return *this;
}
```

For additional information on the implementation of subclass assignment operators see Rule 124.

113. Implement Copy-Safe and Exception-Safe Assignment Operators

Take care that your assignment operators are both copy-safe and exception-safe. For most classes, a self-assignment is rare, but you must design with the assumption that self-assignment may occur.

If your assignment operator performs any operations that may produce an exception, you must also ensure that the assignment operator does not leave either the source or the target object in an invalid state.

For example, consider the following implementation of an assignment operator:

```
class A {
  public:
    A& operator=(const A& that);
  private:
    char* name_;
};


A& A::operator=(const A& that) {
  delete [] name_;
  name_ = new char[strlen(that.name_)+1];
  strcpy(name_,that.name_);
  return *this;
}
```

The preceding implementation is not copy-safe or exception-safe. If a self-assignment occurs, the method would copy the name array after it deletes it; thus, this implementation is not copy-safe. If the new operation were to fail with an exception, the method would leave name_ pointing at deleted and therefore invalid storage; thus, this implementation is not exception-safe.

You can make your assignment operator copy-safe by adding a test for self-assignment:

```
A& A::operator=(const A& that) {
  if (this != &that) {
    delete [] name_;
```

```
   name_ = new char[strlen(that.name_)+1];
   strcpy(name_,that.name_);
 }
 return *this;
}
```

However, this implementation is not exception-safe because the new operation could fail after the method has already deleted name_. To ensure exception safety, you must fully construct the new object state prior to making any assignments. Note that exception-safe code is almost always copy-safe, so you can eliminate the test for self-assignment unless such an occurrence is common and the assignment operation is computationally expensive:

```
A& A::operator=(const A& that) {
  // Construct a complete copy before assignment
  char* temp = new char[strlen(that.name_)+1];
  strcpy(temp,that.name_);
  char* old = name_;
  name_ = temp;
  delete [] old;
  return *this;
}
```

114. Define Binary Operators Outside of a Class

Define binary operators as global functions unless the operator modifies the left-hand operand, in which case implement the operator as a member of the left-hand operand class.

However, you should avoid designing binary operators that modify their operands—convert these operators into unary operators and implement them as members of a class.

You must create a global operator if you want to define a binary operation where the left-hand operand is a built-in type since you obviously cannot define the operator as a member function of the built-in type. For example, if you want to add an integer to a user-defined type you would need a global operator:

```
// Add offset to iter to create a new Iterator.
Iterator operator+(int offset,
                   const Iterator& iter) {
  Iterator newIter(iter);
  NewIter += offset;
  return newIter;
}

// Compiler will know what to do.
// Calls operator+(4,iter1)
Iterator iter2(4+iter1);
```

115. Implement a Boolean Operator in Terms of Its Opposite

Implementing one Boolean comparison operator in terms of its opposite is consistent with two goals: making the meaning of an operator obvious (see Rules 110 and 2), and simplifying code:

```
bool operator==(const A& lhs, const A& rhs) {
  return lhs.equals(rhs);
}

bool operator!=(const A& lhs, const A& rhs) {
  return !operator==(lhs,rhs);
}
```

It is logical for a reader of your code to expect that operator!=() would be consistent with the logical negation of operator==(); when you implement Boolean operators in this way, you guarantee those semantics, even if the implementation of operator==() changes at a later date.

The same could be said for operator+= and operator+, for example.

7.8 Templates

116. Use Templates Instead of Macros to Create Parameterized Code

Macros simply provide a mechanism for text substitution; accordingly, they provide no benefit relative to C++ syntax or type safety. You can use C++ features such as templates to accomplish tasks that traditionally required macros (see Rules 87 and 88).

A common example of parameterized code is a max(a,b) function that returns the larger of two values. To accommodate a variety of types, this function is frequently implemented using a macro similar to this:

```
#define MAX(a,b) (((a) > (b)) ? (a) : (b))
```

However, this macro can produce all sorts of unexpected behavior:[27]

```
int a = 0;
int r;
r = MAX(a++, 0); // a incremented once: r = 0
r = MAX(a++, 0); // a incremented twice: r = 2
```

You can provide a type-safe parameterization of this function using a C++ function template, e.g.,

```
template<class T>
inline T max(const T& a, const T& b) {
```

---

[27] Scott Meyers, *Effective C++: 50 Specific Ways to Improve Your Programs and Design, Second Edition.* (Reading, Massachusetts: Addison-Wesley, 1997), p. 16.

```
  return (a > b) ? a : b;
}
```

This version of max produces the expected results:

```
int a = 0;
int r;
r = max(a++, 0);  // a incremented once: r = 0;
r = max(a++, 0);  // a incremented once: r = 1;
```

117. Do Not Use CV-Qualified Types as Template Parameters

When you instantiate a template with a CV-qualified [const or volatile] type, you may inadvertently violate the semantics and usage requirements of the template. Let the person designing the template determine what CV qualifiers to apply to the parameter type. The following example demonstrates how instantiation with a qualified type produces a compile-time error:

```
template <typename T> class A {
  public:
    A(const T&);
    void foo(T& t);
};

template <typename T>
void A<T>::foo(T& t) {
  t.nonConstMethod();
}

class B {
  public:
    void nonConstMethod(void);
};
```

```
void f() {
  B b;
  A<B> a1(b); // Good! Unqualified type.
  a1.f(b);

  A<const B> a2(b); // Bad! CV-qualified type.
  a2.f(b); // Error!
}
```

The final call, a2.f(b), fails to compile because the compiler is not allowed to cast away const when attempting to convert the const B& parameter of foo() to the B& required to make the call to nonConstMethod().

7.9 Type Safety, Casting, and Conversion

118. *Use C++ Casting Operators Instead of C-style Casts*

The C-style casts allow you to reinterpret almost any value, even though the result may not be what you want or is complete nonsense. In many cases, use of an old-style cast results in a loss of information that the compiler might have used to detect simple coding errors or invalid usage. You may inadvertently ask for an invalid reinterpretation or explicitly give access to memory that falls outside of the its original allocation, give access to a volatile object that has no memory allocation, or give write access to memory that was read-only.

While you can use old-style casts to request intrinsic mathematical type promotion and conversion, you can also use them to request unconstrained reinterpretation at the bit level. The compiler will attempt to do as you ask, even if the interpretation is invalid. An invalid interpretation can often be difficult to locate and may go undetected, at least until reinterpretation produces a value that breaks your software. The most common sorts of casting errors involve reinterpretation of pointers and the accidental removal of const.

Old-style casts also use a notation that relies on parentheses. Because parentheses are used in function declarations, function invocations, and subexpression grouping, an old-style cast is easily overlooked within the source and can be quite difficult to locate using search tools. By using the new-style casting operators (static_cast<>, dynamic_cast<>, etc.), you are able to distinguish and locate explicit casts wherever they occur.

119. *Avoid Type Casting and Do Not Force Others to Use It*

Explicit type casting often circumvents the normal type-safety enforcement mechanisms provided by the C++ language. Casting operations may produce subtle errors that may not be detected until somebody else modifies or extends the types and values you are manipulating.

Let the compiler generate type-safe implicit conversions and use casting operators only as a last resort. The most common exception to this rule is when static_cast<> is used to force type conversion when the choice of implicit conversion is ambiguous, which is often the case when selecting between overloaded functions. You may also choose to use static_cast<> to expose non-intuitive implicit conversions or to perform downcasting; see the next rule.

120. *Use* static_cast<> *to Expose Non-Intuitive Implicit Conversions*

The implicit type conversion and operator overloading features of the C++ language allow you to create elegant designs that hide the complexities of an underlying implementation behind a simple programming interface. Implicit type conversion is often used to reduce the number of functions overloads, especially when there exists a large number of combinatorial permutations.

However, some implicit conversions may be non-intuitive to those reading the code that produces them. Use `static_cast<>` to replace implicit conversions that you suspect are non-intuitive, subtle, or unexpected.

121. *Do Not Use* `reinterpret_cast<>` *in Portable Code*

The `reinterpret_cast<>` operator provides a mechanism for reinterpretation of pointer and integral values. The reinterpretation process is unsafe and the result may be implementation-dependent. This implies that code containing `reinterpret_cast<>` operators may not be portable.

The result of a `reinterpret_cast<>` can only be safely used after casting back to the original type, e.g., `int*` to `char*` back to `int*`. Never use this casting operator to navigate class hierarchies; use `static_cast<>` instead.

You may find that you need to use `reinterpret_cast<>` when interfacing with older or low-level 'C' language libraries. Many such libraries had to rely on a flexible interpretation of storage content to simplify memory management and reduce memory usage. Avoid direct manipulation of library structures if possible—always use the methods provided by the library if they exist.

If you need a design that requires a flexible interpretation of storage, consider using `union` declarations instead of `reinterpret_cast<>`.

122. *Only Use* `const_cast<>` *on* "this" *or When Dealing with Non-Const-Correct Code*

You should always try to avoid any use of `const_cast<>`. When you use this casting operator to change the "const-ness" of an object, you are violating an implicit contract imposed by the producer or consumers of the object.

A common scenario for `const_cast<>` usage arises when you want to hide certain state changes that do not affect the apparent const-ness of an object. In this situation, a `const` method may cast away `const` on `this` to produce a pointer that can be used to perform non-const operations. However, in many such situations, you can avoid the use of `const_cast<>` by declaring the relevant data members using the `mutable` keyword. Another common scenario occurs when somebody else has written code that is not "const correct." It is quite common to find that a third party has declared a function with a pointer or reference to a non-object, when in fact it makes no changes to the value of the referenced object. This is quite common in older C libraries where there are functions that accept non-const character strings when they should instead have accepted constant strings.

123. *Never Use* `dynamic_cast<>` *as a Substitute for Polymorphism*

Do not use `dynamic_cast<>` to select behavior based on object type. Such code may require modification with each addition of a new object type, especially when the new types are subclasses of existing ones (see *Open-Closed Principle* in Rule 61). Those tasked with maintaining your code may not know that any changes are required.

```
// Polymorphic superclass
class Shape {
  // ...
  // But no polymorphic rotation support!
  // ...
};
```

```cpp
class Matrix {
  public:
    void rotate(Shape* shape) const;
};


class Circle : public Shape {
  public:
    Circle& rotate(const Matrix& matrix);
};


class Triangle : public Shape {
  public:
    Triangle& rotate(const Matrix& matrix);
};


// Bad!
void Matrix::rotate(Shape* shape) const {
  // Test for null pointer that results if
  // dynamic_cast<> cannot perform conversion
  if (Circle* circle =
      dynamic_cast<Circle*>(shape)) { // Bad!
    circle->rotate(*this);
  }
  else if(Triangle* triangle =
          dynamic_cast<Triangle*>(shape)) {
    triangle->rotate(*this);
  }
  // Add else-if clause for each new shape
  // here ...
}
```

If you were to add a Rectangle class to the preceding example, you would need to add another else-if block in Matrix::rotate(). You should instead use polymorphism based on virtual functions to select the proper behavior for an object type:

```
class Matrix;

class Shape {
  public:
    virtual Shape& rotate(const Matrix& matrix);
};

class Matrix {
  public:
    void rotate(Shape* shape) const;
};

class Circle : public Shape {
  public:
    virtual Shape& rotate(const Matrix& matrix);
};

class Triangle : public Shape {
  public:
    virtual Shape& rotate(const Matrix& matrix);
};

class Rectangle : public Shape { // New shape!
  public:
    virtual Shape& rotate(const Matrix& matrix);
};

void Matrix::rotate(Shape* shape) const {
// Correct! Rectangle works too!
shape->rotate(*this);
}
```

124. Use `dynamic_cast<>` to Restore Lost Type Information

Use the `dynamic_cast<>` operator to recover type information that is lost when a subclass reference is upcast to a superclass reference. Do not use `dynamic_cast<>` as a substitute for polymorphism (see Rule 123).

The following example shows how you can use `dynamic_cast<>` to define a virtual assignment operator that can handle a situation where the source or target of an assignment has been upcast from `DerivedClass` to `BaseClass`. Note that the standard assignment operator executes the actual assignment—by providing a separate standard assignment operator, we eliminate the overhead of performing an unnecessary `dynamic_cast<>` operation when the compiler already knows that the type of the source and target object is `DerivedClass`:

```cpp
class BaseClass {
  public:
    virtual BaseClass& operator= (const
BaseClass&);
};

BaseClass&
BaseClass::operator=(const BaseClass& b) {
  //...
  return *this;
}

class DerivedClass : public BaseClass {
  public:
    virtual BaseClass&
    operator=(const BaseClass&);
```

```cpp
    DerivedClass&
    operator=(const DerivedClass&);
};

BaseClass&
DerivedClass::operator=(const BaseClass& b) {
  // Try the dynamic_cast<>
  // Use pointers to avoid bad_cast exception
  if (const DerivedClass* dp =
    dynamic_cast<const DerivedClass*>(&b)) {
    // Handle b as reference to DerivedClass...
    return operator=(*dp);
  }
  else {
    // Forward b to BaseClass.
    return BaseClass::operator=(b);
  }
}

DerivedClass&
DerivedClass::operator= (const DerivedClass& d)
{
  //...
  return *this;
}

static void f() {
  BaseClass b1, b2;
  DerivedClass d1, d2;
  BaseClass& d1br = d1;

  // calls BaseClass:: operator=()
  b1 = b2;
  // forwards to BaseClass::operator=()
```

```
    d1 = b1;
    // calls DerivedClass::operator=()
    d1 = d2;
    // forwards to BaseClass::operator=()
    d1br = b1;
    // forwards to DerivedClass::operator=()
    d1br = d2;
}
```

125. *Always Treat String Literals as* const char*

Make sure you never assign or pass string literals to non-const char* pointers. A C++ compiler may allocate and store string literals in static storage, which you cannot modify without producing a runtime exception. However, a C++ compiler does not complain if you treat a string literal as a char*, because C compilers do not prevent this—C++ compilers must adopt the C behavior to maintain compatibility.

126. *Use C++ Streams Instead of* stdio *Functions for Type Safety*

The classic stdio.h I/O functions are not type-safe. Many of these functions are declared using the '...' (vararg) notation that allows them to accept a variable-length, but untyped, list of arguments. In the following example, the compiler accepts the arguments passed to the second printf() statement even though they fail to match the types given in the format string. Most compilers also do not detect whether you have passed enough arguments for the specified format string. A format argument type or count mismatch may still execute, but it produces unexpected results. In many cases, a type mismatch produces fatal memory access exceptions:

```
#include <stdio.h>

void f() {
```

```
    int i = 10;
    const char* s = "Hello";
    // This compiles and produces "10Hello"
    printf("%i%s",i,s);

    // This compiles but will likely produce
    // a fatal exception!
    printf("%i%s",s,i);
}
```

The C++ IOStreams operations are inherently type-safe. Each type must have its own input [extraction] and output [insertion] operator before it can be used in a stream input or output expression. Each such operator recognizes and implements the proper formatting for a value of the associated type. The number and format of input or output values is determined by a sequence of insertion or extraction operators, not by a separate format string:

```
#include <iostream>

void g() {
    int i = 10;
    const char* s = "Hello";

    // This produces "10Hello"
    std::cout << i << s << std::endl;

    // This produces "Hello10"
    std::cout << s << i << std::endl;
}
```

127. Test All Type Conversions

Designs that use conversion constructors, conversion operators, and overloaded functions should always undergo careful testing. Test all supported conversions, and any expressly prohibited conversions, to verify that the compiler finds no unexpected ambiguities or allows any illegal conversions.

7.10 Initialization and Construction

128. Initialize All Variables

The uninitialized variable is one of the most common and insidious of all software defects. Software containing an uninitialized variable may work only because its memory location happens to contain a viable value. This may hold true for years, until a new compilation or invocation order results in code that leaves a different, unexpected value in the variable's memory location.

Most compilers can generate warnings for uninitialized variables; use these warnings to locate and correct these omissions. Some compilers can support debugging of uninitialized variables by filling unused call-stack memory with non-zero values typically consisting of bytes containing alternating bit patterns, e.g., 0xAA and 0x55. These values cause uninitialized variables to take on values that likely produce some sort of failure.

129. Do Not Rely on the Order of Initialization of Global Objects

The C++ language does not specify or provide a means for specifying the order of initialization of static objects defined in separate object modules (compilation units). If you have interdependencies within a set of global static objects, you must initialize that set in a single object module. If you initialize a static class member in a file other than the source file you used to implement that class, add a comment to identify the source file that contains the initialization statement for that member.

Take care that you do not inadvertently create a dependency between one of your own global objects and those provided by third-party libraries.

130. Always Construct Objects in a Valid State

Never allow an invalid object to be constructed. If you implement a constructor that does not produce a valid object because you intend to use it as part of a multistage initialization process, make that constructor protected or private and use a static method to coordinate the construction.

To keep your constructors simple and fast, consider using lazy evaluation to delay initialization (see Rule 160).

131. Initialize Member Variables in the Initializer List

When possible, initialize class member data in the constructor's member initializer list instead of in the body of the constructor. When you initialize a compound object using assignment, you execute both the default constructor and the assignment operator. You should also initialize non-compound members in the initializer list for consistency:

```
class Foo {
  public:
    Foo(void);
    Foo(const Foo& other);
    const Foo& operator=(const Foo&);
};

class Bar {
  public:
    Bar(const Foo& foo);
    Bar(int i, const Foo& foo);
  private:
    int i_;
    Foo foo_;
};

// Bad! Foo() and Foo::operator=() called
Bar::Bar(const Foo& foo) {
```

```
  foo_ = foo;
}
```

```
// Good! Foo(const Foo&) called
Bar::Bar(int i, const Foo& foo)
 :i_(i), foo_(foo) {
}
```

You are, of course, required to initialize references in the initializer list, because you cannot change these members within the body of the constructor.

In some cases, you may also realize better performance when using member initializers to eliminate the construction of additional temporary variables.[28] You also eliminate the risk of using an uninitialized value in the body of the constructor.

132. Initialize Member Variables in the Order They are Declared

A C++ compiler initializes class members in the order you declare them, regardless of how you order your constructor initializer list. Most readers of your code, even experienced C++ programmers, assume that the initializations occur in the order you list them. In most cases, especially in well-designed classes, the order of initialization should not be important, but to avoid errors and confusion, you should always initialize in the order of declaration.

```
class A {
  public:
    A(int i);
```

---

[28] Bjarne Stroustrup, *The C++ Programming Language, Third Edition*. (Reading, Massachusetts: Addison-Wesley, 1997), section 10.4.6.1.

```
private:
    int x_;
    int y_;
    int z_;
};

A::A(int i = 100)
  : y_(i)
  , x_(++y_)
  , z_(++y_) {  // This is not what you want!
}
```

An unsuspecting reader might assume that a default instance would be initialized such that x_==101, y_==102, and z_==101. However, the actual result will be x_==<undefined>, y_==101, and z_==101.

Because the initializers are executed in the order the member variables are declared, x_ gets initialized to ++y_ before y_ has been initialized to i. That is why x_ will likely contain garbage and y_ is incremented only once after initialization to 100.

To avoid confusion, you should always order your member initializers to match the order of the member declarations. You should try to avoid introducing initialization dependencies between members because this would make the order of initialization important. If you decide to change the order of declarations in a class, make sure you also update any constructor initializer lists.

133. Indicate When the Declaration Order of Data Members is Significant

If the order of member initialization is important, add comments to the class and data member declarations to indicate that the order of their declaration is important and should not be changed indiscriminately (see Rule 132).

134. Always List any Superclass Constructors in the Initializer List of a Subclass Constructor

A subclass should not directly initialize a superclass member—superclass member initialization is the responsibility of the superclass constructor. Instead, always include the appropriate superclass constructor in the initializer list, even if it is a default constructor:

```cpp
class Base {
  public:
    Base(int foo);
  protected:
    int foo_;
};

Base::Base(int foo)
  : foo_(foo) {
}

class A : public Base {
  public:
    A(int foo);
};

A::A(int foo) { // Bad! Base() not listed
  foo_ = foo;   // Bad! Let Base do this!
}

class B : public Base {
  public:
    B(void);
    B(int foo);
};
```

```
B::B(void)
  : Base() {     // Good!
}

B::B(int foo)
  : Base(foo) { // Good!
}
```

135. Do Not Call Virtual Functions in Constructors and Destructors

You cannot use the virtual function dispatch mechanism to call functions in a subclass from within a superclass constructor or destructor.[29] This is because the compiler-generated code initializes the virtual function dispatch table from the top down, starting at the superclass and proceeding down the class hierarchy to the immediate class of the object. Any attempt to call a virtual function within a class constructor can only result in a call to the function implementation in that class or one of its superclasses—you cannot invoke a subclass method from within a superclass constructor because any subclass virtual function overrides are incorporated into the function dispatch table until the subclass portion of the object initialization is complete.

The same restriction holds true for destructors. The compiler-generated code invokes object destructors in the order opposite that of construction. This means that the virtual functions associated with a subclass are no longer accessible once the subclass destructor has executed.

While there may be occasions where you might anticipate or exploit this behavior, you should still avoid calling virtual

---

[29] G. Bowden Wise. "The ABCs of Writing C++ Classes," Guideline #12. http://www.cs.rpi.edu/~wiseb/xrds/ovp1-4.html.

functions from within your constructors, because this may produce confusion for any others who must look at your code. If your constructor requires functionality provided by a virtual function, create a separate, non-virtual method that provides that functionality and call that function from your constructor and virtual function.

136. Declare and Initialize Static Variables within Functions

Your program initializes any static variables that you declare within a function body the first time a thread enters the function.[30] This is a form of *lazy evaluation* (see Rule 160). You can use this behavior to improve the performance of your application by delaying the construction of non-trivial static objects until they are required.

You can use a function-scope static variable to implement a simple singleton pattern:[31]

```
NonTrivialClass* getSingleton(void) {
  static NonTrivialClass singleton;
  return &singleton;
}
```

Unfortunately, this form of initialization may not be multithread-safe. Few compilers ensure that the first-entry test is an atomic operation. This means that it is possible to have more than one thread attempt to initialize a variable. More importantly, other threads may try to use a variable before the first thread that entered the function has finished initializing the variable.

---

[30] Timothy Budd. *C++ for Java Programmers*. (Reading, Massachusetts: Addison-Wesley, 1999), p. 204.
[31] Erich Gamma et al. *Design Patterns: Elements of Reusable Object-Oriented Software*. (Reading, Massachusetts: Addison-Wesley, 1994), pp. 127–134.

137. Zero Pointers after Deletion

After using a pointer to delete an object or to free storage, set that pointer to zero. This helps make memory management errors much more obvious, because any attempt to dereference a null pointer generates an exception, whereas an attempt to dereference a stale pointer may not generate any errors and may prove to be a serious defect that is difficult to detect.

138. Use the new and delete Operators Instead of malloc() and free()

The C++ new and delete operators are for management of objects, whereas the C-style malloc() and free() functions are for management of uninitialized memory. Specifically, free() does not force destructors to be invoked.

When allocating and deallocating memory for an array, use operators new[] and delete[].

7.11 Statements and Expressions

139. Do Not Rely on Operator Precedence in Complex Expressions

Complex expressions are difficult to visually parse and understand, especially those that rely on operator precedence for subexpression evaluation and ordering. You and any future maintainers can easily make mistakes when coding or modifying expressions that rely on operator precedence. Use parentheses to define and control the evaluation of subexpressions. This makes your code easier to understand and easier to maintain:

```
// Trying to get 60
int j = 10 * 2 << 1 + 20; // Bad! j == 41943040

// Add some parentheses ...
j = (10 * (2 << 1)) + 20; // Good! j == 60
```

```
// Write value of 2^8
// Bad! Writes '18'
cout << 1L << 8L << endl;

// Add some parentheses ...
// Good! Writes '256'
cout << ( 1L << 8L ) << endl;
```

140. Use Block Statements in Control Flow Constructs

The compound or block statement provides a mechanism for treating any number of statements as a single compound statement. A block statement may be used anywhere a regular statement may be used. The various C++ control flow statements, if..else, for, while, and do..while, provide the means for conditionally executing a simple or compound statement.

You must use block statements if you wish to conditionally execute multiple statements as part of a control flow statement. You may also need to use block statements when nesting if..else statements to avoid a potential ambiguity often referred to as the "dangling else problem."

```
if (x >= 0)
  if (x > 0) positiveX();
else // This clause matches most recent if!
  negativeX();

if (x >= 0) {
  if (x > 0) positiveX();
}
else {
  negativeX(); // Good! What we wanted!
}
```

When you use block statements, you make it easier to add additional statements to an existing control flow construct:

```
for (int i = n; i >= 0; i--)
  for (int j = n; j >= 0; j--)
    f(i,j);
    g(i,j); // Bad! Cannot add here!

for (int i = n;i >= 0;i--) {
  for (int j = n;j >= 0;j--) {
    f(i,j);
    g(i,j); // Good! Can add here!
  }
}
```

If a control statement has a single, trivial statement as its body, you may put the entire statement on a single line, but only if it improves readability. Treat this case as the exception rather than the norm.

141. Do Not Test for Equality with True

When a pointer or numeric value is used in a Boolean expression, a value of zero is treated as `false` while any non-zero value is treated as `true`. When the built-in Boolean constants are evaluated as integers, the constant `false` has a value of zero while `true` usually has a value of one. When a pointer or numeric value is tested for equality with `true`, both values are interpreted as integers—the comparison returns `true` only if the pointer or numeric value is equal to the integer representation of `true`.

Always evaluate pointer or numeric values as Boolean or test for inequality with `false` or zero rather than testing for equality with `true`:

```
int i = 10;
int* ip;
```

```
// Test for non-zero i
if (i == true) {} // Bad! (May produce warning)
if (i != false) {} // OK, but not great
if (i) {}           // Better
if (i != 0) {}      // Best!

// Test for null pointer
if (ip != true) {} // Bad! (May not compile)
if (ip == false) {} // OK.
if (!ip) {}         // Better
if (ip == 0) {}     // Best!
```

142. Replace Repeated, Non-Trivial Expressions with Equivalent Methods

As you write code, look for repeated expressions or operations that might be factored into separate methods.

When you replace factored code with a function call, you simplify and reduce the size of the code. This makes your code easier to read.

When you replace factored code with a meaningful function name, you improve the self-documenting quality of your code. This makes your code easier to understand.

When you factor code into a single method, you simplify testing by localizing behavior, and maintenance by localizing change.

143. Use `size_t` Variables for Simple Loop Iteration and Array Subscripts

Use `size_t` for array indices because `size_t` is the type produced when measuring the size of an array using `sizeof()`. It is also the type used to specify the allocation size in the operator `new()` functions.

While the size and maximum value of the size_t type is implementation defined, it is guaranteed to be large enough to index any dynamically, automatically, or statically allocated array.

By using size_t you eliminate the possibility that your implementation would leave part of an array out of reach. For example,

```
assert(sizeof(size_t) > sizeof(short));

// size_t is 32 bits
const size_t len = 0xFFFFFFFF;
double x[len];

// initialize array
for (short i = 0; i < len; i++) { // Bad!
  x[i] = 1.0;
}
```

The code in this example would attempt to access storage outside of the array when the short index variable overflows to become a negative number. Changing the index variable to unsigned short eliminates the illegal memory access error, but leaves the upper half of the array uninitialized and results in an infinite loop because the index overflows back to zero. (Fortunately, most compilers warn you about comparing a signed value with an unsigned one. Don't disregard these warnings too hastily!)

144. Use a Dummy Template Function to Eliminate Warnings for Unused Variables

Many RAII implementations rely on block-scope objects for resource management. These objects may never be accessed after construction. If the compiler detects that your code does not reference such an object, it produces a warning message for an "unreferenced variable." You can eliminate this warning by casting the variable to void using static_cast<>, but this method does not make for very readable code. You can improve the readability of your code and can also eliminate the warning by referencing the variable with an inline template function:

```
template <typename Variable>
void ignoreUnusedVariable(Variable dummy) {
}

void MyClass::function(void) {
  Lock lock(mutex_);            // RAII object
  static_cast<void>(lock);      // Just OK
  ignoreUnusedVariable(lock);   // Good!
}
```

7.12 Control Flow

When we look at a piece of code, we usually begin with the assumption that the statements within that code are executed sequentially. While control flow statements may select different statements or blocks of statements for execution, we still expect control flow to enter a block at the first statement and exit the block after the last—we assume that each block has a single entry and exit point. The software development community has long considered it good programming practice to write code that follows this model. Code written in this manner is often easier to debug because we need only look for a single exit point instead of many.

A C++ programmer can subvert this model of control flow by using the goto, break, continue, return, and throw statements. While many situations exist where use of these statements is recommended or even mandatory, these statements are often used in a manner that makes code harder to read, understand, test, and maintain.

145. *Avoid* break *and* continue *in Iteration Statements*

The break and continue statements interrupt the normal flow of execution. The break statement immediately exits the nearest enclosing iteration statement and all intervening blocks and resumes execution in the statement that follows. The continue statement immediately jumps to the controlling expression of the nearest enclosing iteration statement, exiting all intervening blocks. Both statements produce behavior similar to that of the goto statement.

A reader can easily overlook occurrences of these statements if the enclosing iteration block is large or complex. A reader might also pair a break or continue with the wrong iteration statement and thereby misinterpret the code. Blocks that have multiple exit points are more difficult to debug since a separate breakpoint may be required at each exit point.

Try using a combination of if..else statements and controlling expressions to produce the behavior that you might otherwise get if you used break and continue. However, you may choose to ignore this rule if you find that you must create and evaluate a number of additional state variables or complex expressions just to avoid use of these statements.[32] The cost in complexity and performance may override style considerations. If you do choose to use break or continue statements, add obvious comments to highlight these special exit points.

146. *Avoid Multiple* return *Statements in Functions*

When used anywhere but the last statement in a function block, a return statement also interrupts normal execution

---

[32] Steve McConnell. *Code Complete*. (Redmond, Washington: Microsoft Press, 1993), pp. 337–338.

flow. A reader typically looks for the return statement at the end of a function, so if you place them in other locations, add obvious comments to highlight these other exit points.

147. Do Not Use goto

The use of goto is one of the great religious arguments in computer programming, originally brought to the forefront by Edsger Dijkstra's famous essay, "Go To Statement Considered Harmful."[33]

While goto statements may have a place in programming languages without powerful control constructs, suffice it to say that if you think that you need to use a goto in C++, you may be doing something wrong[34] (but sometimes not[35]).

148. Do Not Use try..throw..catch to Manage Control Flow

You should only use the C++ exception mechanism to handle exceptional conditions. Do not use it as a substitute for normal controlling conditions in if..else, for, while, and do..while or control flow statements such as return, break, and continue.

149. Never Use setjmp() or longjmp() in a C++ Program

These functions provide exception handling for C programs. You cannot safely use these functions in C++ code because the

[33] Edsger W. Dijkstra. "Go To Statement Considered Harmful," Communications of the ACM, Vol. 11, No. 3 (Mar 1968), pp. 147–148.
[34] Timothy Budd. C++ for Java Programmers. (Reading, Massachusetts: Addison-Wesley, 1999), pp. 209–210.
[35] Steve McConnell. Code Complete. (Redmond, Washington: Microsoft Press, 1993), section 16.1, pp. 347–359.

exception-handling mechanism they implement does not respect normal object lifecycle semantics—a jump will not result in destruction of scoped, automatically allocated objects.[36]

Always use the `try..throw..catch` C++ exception handling mechanism instead of `setjmp()` and `longjmp()`.

150. *Always Code a* `break` *Statement in the Last Case of a Switch Statement*

The following switch statement was coded with the assumption that no other cases would follow the `Y` case, so no `break` statement was inserted:

```
switch ( ... ) {
  case X:
    // ...
    break;
  case Y:
    // ...
    // Should have placed a break here!
}
```

What if a new case is needed? The person adding this case may simply decide to add it after the last case, but may fail to notice that the last case did not have a `break` statement. This person may inadvertently introduce a hard-to-detect "fall-through" error, as shown here:

```
switch ( ... ) {
  case X:
    // ...
    break;
```

---

[36] Timothy Budd. *C++ for Java Programmers*. (Reading, Massachusetts: Addison-Wesley, 1999), pp. 182–184.

```
  case Y:
    // ...
    // Oops! Unintended fall-through!
  case Z:
    // ...
}
```

In anticipation of future changes, you should always code a break statement in the last case in the switch statement, even if it is the default case:

```
switch (...) {
  case W:
    // ...
    // Falls through to next case!
  case X:
    // ...
    break;
  case Y:
    // ...
    break; // OK! No more fall-through!
  case Z:
    // ...
    break;
  default:
    // ...
    break; // Consistent.
}
```

Do not forget to add a "fall-through" comment in those cases where you do want to leave out the break statement (see Rule 53).

7.13 Error and Exception Handling

151. *Use Return Codes to Report Expected State Changes*

For expected state changes, use a return code, sentinel, or method to report expected state changes. This makes code more readable and the flow of control straightforward. For example, in the course of reading from a file, it is expected that the end of the file will be reached at some point—do not use an exception to report the end-of-file.

152. *Use Assertions to Enforce a Programming Contract*

Use *precondition* assertions to test the validity of the arguments passed to a method or test that the associated object is in a valid state when that method is called.

Use *postcondition* assertions to test the validity of the results produced by the method or test that the associated object is in a valid state before method returns.

153. *Do Not Silently Absorb or Ignore Unexpected Runtime Errors*

To create robust software, you need to identify potential sources of runtime errors. If there is any possibility of recovering from the error, you should do so, or at least give your client the opportunity to do so.

Always verify that an operation has completed successfully. If a method returns an indication that it has failed you should determine the cause for the failure and take appropriate action. Use error query functions such as `errno()` or `GetLastError()`, `try..catch` blocks, and error callback functions to detect and respond to errors.

If you detect an unrecoverable error, use an assertion or exception to report the error (see Rule 154). If you have access to some form of execution logging facility, log the cause, type, and location of the error prior to taking other action.

154. Use Assertions to Report Unexpected or Unhandled Runtime Errors

You are seldom able to anticipate or recover from all runtime errors. Some errors, such as hardware, third-party software, or internal program logic errors are so severe that no recovery is possible. Program termination may be your only recourse.

You may decide to throw an exception for unexpected runtime errors in a release build of your software, but you should use assertions in debug builds. An assertion produces a message that indicates the location of the failure, and breaks execution when running in a debugger, thereby preserving information about the call stack. You lose this information if you use an exception.

Check all assumptions that your code makes. For example, use `assert()` to check for unexpected null pointers, unexpected states, out-of-bounds indices, illegal sizes, and so on.

Only use assertions to check for unexpected or unrecoverable errors. If the caller can recover from an error condition, the code should return an error code or throw an exception.

Since the expressions used in assertion macros are only compiled in debug builds, you should never use "live" code—code that produces side effects—inside these expressions.

155. Use Exceptions to Report Errors That May Occur Under Normal Program Execution

Use exceptions to report unexpected but potentially recoverable errors. Some typical examples include the following:

—A file write operation failed because the disk was full.

—A file access operation failed because the disk was removed or unmounted.

—The system could not satisfy a memory-allocation request.

—The system communication software encountered an invalid protocol, sequence, or format.

—A communication request or response was unexpectedly interrupted or canceled by a client.

156. *Manage Resources with RAII for Exception Safety*

In cases where it is critical that your code release a recently acquired resource, such as dynamically allocated memory or thread synchronization lock, use the RAII technique. The RAII technique relies on the construction and destruction of automatically allocated objects to peform resource acquisition and release—the constructor of an RAII object acquires a resource and the destructor releases it.

RAII objects provide an exception-safe means for resource management because these objects are declared with block scope and are therefore guaranteed to be destroyed upon block exit, even if that exit occurs as a result of a `throw` (see also Rule 102). RAII objects also simplify resource management for users of your code—they need not remember to release a resource once it has been acquired.

Consider the following implementation of a `Mutex` and related RAII `Lock` class:

```
class Mutex {
  public:
    Mutex(void);
    void acquire(void);
    void release(void);

    class Lock { // Provides RAII-based locking
```

```
      public:
        Lock(Mutex& mutex);
        ~Lock();
      private:
        Mutex& mutex_;
 };
};

Mutex::Lock::Lock(Mutex& mutex)
  : mutex_(mutex) {
  mutex_.acquire();
}

Mutex::Lock::~Lock() {
  mutex_.release();
}

class A {
  public:
    void method(void);
  private:
    Mutex mutex_;
};

void A::method(void) {
  Mutex::Lock lock(mutex_);
  // ...
  if (error) throw std::exception();
  // ...
  // lock destruction will release mutex
}
```

157. *Catch Exceptions by Reference, Not by Value*

The C++ standard does not dictate the internal mechanisms
that a compiler must use to store and propagate exceptions,

but nearly all compilers copy an exception object if it is caught by value. The following code demonstrates this behavior:

```cpp
class Exception {
  public:
    Exception(void);
    Exception(const Exception& other);
    ~Exception();
  private:
    int index_;
    static int count_;
}

int Exception::count_ = 0;

Exception::Exception(void)
  : index_(count_++) {
  cout << "Constructed #" << index_ << endl;
}

Exception::Exception(const Exception& other)
  : index_(count_++) {
  cout << "Constructed #" << index_
       << "from #" << other.index_ << endl;
}

Exception::~Exception() {
  cout << "Destroyed #" << index_ << endl;
}

void thrower(void) {
  throw Exception();
}

void byValueCatcher(void) {
```

```
  try {
    thrower();
}
catch(Exception e) { // Bad! Produces copy!
  // ...
  }
}
```

A call to byValueCatcher() produces the following output:

```
Constructed #0
Constructed #1 from #0
Destroyed #1
Destroyed #2
```

As you can see, the exception constructed by thrower()
was copied when caught in byValueCatcher(). To eliminate this unnecessary copy, catch the exception as a const
reference:

```
void byReferenceCatcher(void) {
  try {
    thrower();
  }
  catch(const Exception& e) { // Good!
    // ...
  }
}
```

The catch clause in this function does not produce a copy, as
demonstrated by the output it produces:

```
Constructed #0
Destroyed #0
```

158. Do Not Discard Exception Information if You Throw a New Exception Within a `catch` *Block*

When you throw a new exception within a `catch()` block, use your exception to augment the information supplied in the original exception. If you simply ignore the information provided by the exception you caught, you discard information that might prove valuable at a higher level (see Rule 153).

There are several approaches to retaining the information from the original exception. You might, for example, concatenate your exception message text to that contained in the original exception. You might also consider carrying a copy of the original exception as a member of your exception. The following example shows how you can use a template to provide this functionality:

```
class ExceptionBase : public std::runtime_error
{
  public:
    ExceptionBase(const std::string& message);
    virtual void rethrow(void) const = 0;
};

// ...

template <typename Original>

class Exception : public ExceptionBase {
  public:
    Exception(const std::string& message,
              const Original& original);
    virtual void rethrow(void) const;
  private:
    Original original_;
};
```

```cpp
template <typename Original>
Exception<Original>::
Exception(const std::string& message,
          const Original& original)
  : ExceptionBase(message)
  , original_(original) {
}


template <typename Original>
void Exception<Original>::rethrow(void) const {
  throw original_;
}


// Recursively prints nested exception
// messages
void dump(const ExceptionBase& current) {
  std::cout << current.what() << std::endl;
  try {
    current.rethrow();
  }
  catch (const ExceptionBase& e) {
   // Recursively dump nested exceptions
   dump(e);
  }
  catch (const std::exception& e) {
    std::cout << e.what() << std::endl;
  }
}


// Throws initial exception
static void thrower(void) {
    if (error)
        throw std::domain_error ("thrower");
}
```

```
// catches then throws new exception
void rethrower(void) {
  try {
    thrower();
  }
  catch (const std::domain_error& e) {
    throw
    Exception<std::domain_error>("rethrow", e);
  }
}

void catcher(void) {
  try {
    rethrower();
  }
  catch (const ExceptionBase& e) {
    dump(e); // "Unwinds" nested exceptions
  }
}
```

159. *Avoid Throwing Exceptions in Destructors*

Since automatic objects are destroyed at scope exit, there is no natural place to catch any exceptions that might be thrown by their destructors.

In addition, should an exception be thrown from a destructor while another exception is in progress, the program would call terminate() and promptly die.

7.14 Efficiency

160. *Use Lazy Evaluation and Initialization*

Do not perform a complex calculation until you need the result. Always perform calculations at the most nested scope possible. If possible, cache the result.

This concept can be applied to object construction and initialization as well—do not construct an object that you may not use until you need it. Access the object using a simple dedicated function. This function must construct the object the first time you call it and return a reference to the object from that point on. Any code that requires access to the object must use that function. Serialization (locking) may be required to prevent concurrent initialization. In the following example, we assume that a LoanCalculator is an object we do not want to build unless we have to:

```cpp
class LoanCalculator {
  // ...
};

class PersonalFinance {
  public:
    PersonalFinance(void);
    ~PersonalFinance();
  private:
    LoanCalculator* getLoanCalculator();
    LoanCalculator* loanCalculator_;
};

PersonalFinance::PersonalFinance(void)
  : loanCalculator_(0){
}

PersonalFinance::~PersonalFinance() {
  delete loanCalculator_;
}

LoanCalculator*
PersonalFinance::getLoanCalculator(void) {
  // Use double-check pattern to prevent
  // concurrent construction.
```

```
if (loanCalculator_ != 0) {
  // Acquire lock here ...
  if (loanCalculator_ != 0) {
    loanCalculator_ = new LoanCalculator();
  }
  // Release lock here ...
}
return loanCalculator_;
}
```

161. Reuse Objects to Avoid Reallocation

Cache and reuse frequently created objects that have limited life spans.

Use accessor methods instead of constructors to reinitialize the object.

Use a factory implementation to encapsulate mechanisms for caching and reusing objects. To manage these mechanisms properly, you must return objects obtained from an object factory back to the same factory. This means that the association between an object and its factory must be maintained somewhere:

- In the class—a single static factory is associated with the class of the object, and that factory manages all objects of that class.
- In the object—the object maintains a reference to the factory that manages it.
- In the owner of the object—an "owner" of an object maintains a reference to the factory from which the object was obtained.

Take care to choose an implementation that does not need to create its own objects to manage the objects being cached. This would defeat the purpose!

162. Leave Optimization for Last

First Rule of Optimization:

> *Do not do it.*

Second Rule of Optimization (For experts only):

> *Do not do it yet.*
> —*Michael Jackson, Michael Jackson Systems Ltd.*

Do not spend time optimizing code until you are sure you need to do it.

Apply the 80–20 rule:[37] 20 percent of the code in a system uses 80 percent of the resources (on average). If you are going to optimize, make sure you start with code in the 20 percent portion.

---

[37] Steve McConnell. *Code Complete*. (Redmond, Washington: Microsoft Press, 1993), pp. 681–682.

8.

Packaging

Conventions

The C++ standard has nothing to say about the "packaging" of software components or products. You might use namespaces to delineate packages but the namespace mechanism does not govern how a product might be organized, managed, built, or delivered. Consequently, we use the term package rather loosely to refer to any collection of software components that form a non-divisible or deliverable product. A package might take the form of a single source file, a namespace, a library, a framework, or an application.

8.1 Scoping

163. Use Unnamed Namespaces Instead of static *to Hide Local Functions and Variables*

The meaning of the keyword static is quite overloaded in C++. It is used to

- Declare a *class variable*.
- Indicate that the value of a variable should be maintained through all invocations of a function.
- Indicate that file-scope identifiers should have no external linkage.

142 THE ELEMENTS OF C++ STYLE

You can now use unnamed namespaces instead of static to
hide identifiers and provide internal linkage:

```cpp
// global.cpp

// Define global variable
int variable;

// Define global function
void function(void) {
  // Global implementation...
}

// static.cpp
// Define variable without external linkage
static int variable;         // Old style!

// Define local function without
// external linkage
static void function(void) {  // Old style!
  // Local implementation...
}

// namespace.cpp

namespace {                   // Good!
  // Define local variable
  int variable;               // Good!

  // Define local function
  void function(void) {       // Good!
    // Local implementation...
  }
}
```

164. Tread Lightly on the Global Namespace

Classes are themselves worthy namespaces for scoping globally accessible variables. For example, do not do this:

```
class RWMethodType {
  // ...
};


RWMethodType rwType1Method;
RWMethodType rwType2Method;
```

Do this instead:

```
class RWMethodType {
  static RWMethodType type1;
  static RWMethodType type2;
};
```

8.2 Organization

165. Place Types That are Commonly Used, Changed, and Released Together, or Mutually Dependent on Each Other, into the Same Package

This rule encompasses several related package design principles, originally identified by Robert Martin.[38]

The Common Reuse Principle

> A package consists of classes you reuse together.
>
> If you use one of the classes in the package, you use all of them.

---

[38] Robert Martin. "Engineering Notebook: Granularity," C++ Report, Vol. 8, No. 10 (Nov 1996), pp. 57–62.

Place classes and interfaces you usually use together into the same package. Such classes are so closely coupled you cannot use one class without usually using the other. Some examples of closely related types include

- Containers and iterators;
- Database tables, rows, and columns;
- Calendars, dates, and times;
- Points, lines, and polygons.

The Common Closure Principle

> A package consists of classes, all closed against the same kind of changes. A change that affects the package affects all the classes in that package.

Combine classes that are likely to change at the same time, for the same reasons, into a single package. If two classes are so closely related that changing one of them usually involves changing the other, then place them in the same package.

The Reuse-Release Equivalence Principle

> The unit of reuse is the unit of release. Effective reuse requires tracking of releases from a change control system. The package is the effective unit of reuse and release.

Treating individual classes as a unit of release is not very practical. A typical application may consist of tens or hundreds of classes, so releasing code on a class-by-class basis dramatically complicates the integration and testing process and dramatically increases the overall rate of change within the software.

A package provides a much more convenient mechanism for releasing several classes and interfaces. Each class or interface within a package may undergo several independent revisions between releases, but a package release captures only the latest version of each class and interface. Use packages as the primary unit of release and distribution.

The Acyclic Dependencies Principle

> The dependency structure between packages must be a directed acyclic graph; there must be no cycles in the dependency structure.

If two packages directly or indirectly depend on each other, you cannot independently release one without releasing the other because changes in one package often force changes in the other. Such cyclic dependencies dramatically increase the fragility of a system and can eliminate any reduction in schedule realized by assigning the development of each package to separate developers or teams.

Take steps to eliminate cyclic dependencies, either by combining the mutually dependent packages or by introducing a new package of abstractions that both packages can depend on instead of each other.

166. Isolate Unstable Classes in Separate Packages

Avoid placing unstable classes in the same package with stable classes. If you use packages as your principal unit of release and distribution, users can gain access to the latest changes in the unstable classes only if you re-release the entire package. Each time you release the package, your users must absorb the cost of reintegrating and retesting against all the classes in the package, although many may not have changed.

Separate unstable classes from stable classes to reduce the code footprint affected by new releases of code, thereby reducing the impact on users of that code.

167. Avoid Making Difficult-to-Change Packages Dependent on Packages That are Easy to Change

This rule derives from the following design principle.[39]

The Stable Dependencies Principle

> The dependencies between packages should be oriented in the direction of increasing stability. A package should only depend on packages more stable than it is.

If a package containing difficult-to-change types is dependent on a package that contains easy, or likely to change, types, then the dependent package effectively acts to impede change in the volatile package.

In a software system, especially one that is incrementally developed, some packages always remain somewhat volatile. The developers of such a system must feel free to modify and extend these volatile packages to complete the implementation of the system and must be able to do so without worrying too much about downstream effects.

Do not create a package that depends on less-stable packages. If necessary, create new abstractions that can be used to invert the relationship between the stable code and the unstable code.

168. Maximize Abstraction to Maximize Stability

This rule derives from the following design principle.[40]

The Stable Abstractions Principle

> The stability exhibited by a package is directly proportional to its level of abstraction. The more abstract a

---

[39] Robert Martin. "Engineering Notebook: Stability," C++ Report, Vol. 9, No. 2 (Feb 1997).
[40] Ibid.

package is, the more stable it tends to be. The more concrete a package is, the more unstable it tends to be.

Use stable abstractions to create stable packages. Capture high-level, stable concepts in abstract classes and interfaces and provide implementations using concrete classes. Separate abstract classes and interfaces from the concrete classes to form stable and unstable packages. This ensures that the derived classes in the unstable packages depend on the abstract superclasses and interfaces in the stable packages.

169. Capture High-Level Design and Architecture as Stable Abstractions Organized into Stable Packages

To plan and manage a software development effort successfully, the top-level design must stabilize quickly and remain that way. No development manager can hope to accurately plan, estimate, schedule, and allocate resources if the architecture of the system continues to change.

Once the design of the high-level architecture is complete, use packages to separate the stable parts of the design from the volatile implementation. Create packages to capture the high-level abstractions of the design. Place the detailed implementation of those abstractions into separate packages that depend on the high-level abstract packages.

8.3 Files

170. Use the Class Name as the File Name

In general, put only one public class in each file and give the file the same name as the class. Put the class definition in a file named Classname.h, and the class implementation in a file named Classname.cpp (or Classname.cc or Classname.cxx, depending on your organization's standards).

Modern development environments make it easier to find classes and navigate through files; nonetheless, establishing parallel naming for classes and files generally makes things easier for development teams, particularly larger ones.

See also Rule 171.

171. Use Separate Files for Each Namespace-Scope class, struct, union, enumeration, *Function, or Overloaded Function Group*

Give each file the same name as the element it contains, using the same case. Consider also using separate files for template specializations.

Doing this has several benefits. Having elements managed with a high level of granularity frequently simplifies packaging decisions. It becomes easier to locate declarations and implementations without relying on a tool. File contention for source code checkout, editing, and merging by multiple development team members is frequently reduced; the footprint and size of files affected by changes is also reduced, thereby shortening rebuild times. Note finally that this matches the approach taken by most Java™ programmers, which may be an advantage in mixed-language development environments.

172. Use #include *Sparingly in Header Files*

Do not #include a file within a header file unless necessary. If the header does not use a member of a contained or referred class, then you need not #include the header file for the class. Instead, simply declare the external class name as a forward declaration. In large programs, the cumulative effect can speed up compilation dramatically, because the header file for the other class (and any other header files *it* includes) are not read and compiled (see also Rule 109).

```
// Do not #include OtherClass.h definition when
// a forward declaration is sufficent!
```

```
class OtherClass;

class MyClass {
  private:
  // OtherClass not accessed
  OtherClass *other_;
};
```

173. Implement Class Methods Outside of Their Class Declaration Block

Class declarations that include method implementations are more difficult to read, especially in the presence of embedded documentation. The statements that make up a method implementation are more likely to extend past a right margin if you follow proper indentation guidelines.

Use a class declaration block to declare and document each method, not implement them. Define the implementation of any inline methods immediately following the class declaration block. Implement any non-inline functions in a separate source code file.

Separating the implementation from the declaration can help eliminate many circular class-declaration dependency problems—the declaration of a dependent class can be included between a class definition and any methods that would otherwise attempt to use the dependent class before its declaration was complete.

174. Do not Name Files Containing Tests or Examples the Same as Template Header File Names

For example, if you have a template in slist.h, with an accompanying slist.cc implementation file, do not write a test program in a file called slist.cpp. Some compilers try to use the slist.cpp file for the implementation file and everything just goes to heck.

175. Do not Put Global-Scope using or using namespace Declarations in a Header File

Many programmers are tempted to place using declarations in their header files to avoid the need to qualify namespace-scoped names. Unfortunately, in doing so, you impose that decision on everybody who is including your header file. The declarations you import from a namespace may conflict with those in the code that includes your header file.

Feel free to code using declarations within your own namespaces or .cpp files where they do not affect the code of others, but fully qualify the names in your header files.

As Bjarne Stroustrup says, "It is often a good idea to keep local synonyms as local as possible to avoid confusion."[41]

---

[41] Bjarne Stroustrup. *The C++ Programming Language, Third Edition.* (Reading, Massachusetts: Addison-Wesley, 1997), p. 170.

Summary

2. General Principles

1. *Adhere to the style of the original*
2. *Adhere to the Principle of Least Astonishment*
3. *Do it right the first time*
4. *Document any deviations*

3. Formatting Conventions

5. *Use indented block statements*
6. *Indent statements after a label*
7. *Choose one style for brace placement*
8. *Break long statements into multiple lines*
9. *Include white space*
10. *Do not use "hard" tabs*

4. Naming Conventions

11. *Use UPPERCASE and underscores for preprocessor macro names*
12. *Add a unique prefix to macro names*
13. *Use "UpperCamelCase" for classes, constants, structures, enumerations, and typedefs*
14. *Use nouns to name compound types*

15. *Pluralize the names of collections*

16. *Use "lowerCamelCase" for function names*

17. *Use verbs to name functions*

18. *Use "`is`", "`set`", and "`get`" to name accessor and mutator functions*

19. *Use "lowerCamelCase" for variable and function parameter names*

20. *Use nouns to name variables*

21. *Add a prefix or suffix to member variable names to distinguish them from other variables*

22. *Name all function parameters*

23. *Use "`other`" for parameter names in copy constructors and assignment operators*

24. *Give function parameters the same name as the member variables you assigned them to*

25. *Use meaningful names*

26. *Use familiar names*

27. *Avoid the use of digits within names*

28. *Avoid excessively long names*

29. *Join the vowel generation—use complete words*

30. *Use "lowerCamelCase" for abbreviations*

31. *Do not use case to differentiate names*

5. Documentation Conventions

32. *Document your software interface for those who must use it*

33. *Document your implementation for those who must maintain it*

34. *Keep your comments and code synchronized*

35. *Embed API reference documentation in your source code*

36. *Generate API reference documentation directly from the source code*

37. *Document all significant software elements*

38. *Document software elements as early as possible*

39. *Use block comments to describe the programming interface*

40. *Use one-line comments to explain implementation details*

41. *Use a single consistent format and organization for all documentation comments*

42. *Provide a summary description of every declared element*

43. *Document the interface exposed by every function*

44. *Document thread synchronization requirements*

45. *Provide examples to illustrate common and proper usage*

46. *Document important preconditions, postconditions, and invariant conditions*

47. *Document known defects and deficiencies*

48. *Use the active voice to describe actors and passive voice to describe actions*

49. *Use "this" rather than "the" when referring to instances of the current class*

50. *Explain why the code does what it does*

51. *Avoid the use of end-line comments*

52. *Label closing braces in highly nested control structure*

53. *Add a "fall-through" comment between two* case *labels if no* break *statement separates those labels*

54. *Use keywords to mark pending work, unresolved issues, defects, and bug fixes*

6. Programming Principles

55. *Do not be afraid to do engineering*
56. *Choose simplicity over elegance*
57. *Do not use a feature of C++ just "because it is there"*
58. *Recognize the cost of reuse*
59. *Program by contract*
60. *Keep classes simple*
61. *Define subclasses so they may be used anywhere their superclasses may be used*
62. *Use inheritance for "is a" relationships and containment for "has a" relationships*
63. *Avoid multiple inheritance*
64. *Design for reentrancy*
65. *Use threads only where appropriate*
66. *Avoid unnecessary synchronization*
67. *Do not synchronize access to code that does not change shared state*

7. Programming Conventions

68. *Use '#include "..."' for collocated header files and '#include <...>' for external header files*
69. *Place preprocessor include guards in header files*
70. *Use #if..#endif and #ifdef..#endif instead of "/*...*/" comments to hide blocks of code*
71. *Use macros sparingly*

72. *Add a semicolon after every statement expression macro*

73. *Use macros to capture the current file name and line number*

74. *Do not use* "#define" *to define constants—declare* static const *variables instead*

75. *Use portable types for portable code*

76. *Use typedefs to simplify complicated type expressions*

77. *Create a zero-valued enumerator to indicate an uninitialized, invalid, unspecified, or default state*

78. *Do not define enumerations using macros or integer constants*

79. *Declare enumerations within a namespace or class*

80. *Declare global functions, variables, or constants as static members of a class*

81. *Declare for-loop iteration variables inside of* for *statements*

82. *Use an enumeration instead of a Boolean to improve readability*

83. *Use an object pointer instead of a reference if a function stores a reference or pointer to the object*

84. *Accept objects by reference and primitive or pointer types by value*

85. *Use a* const char* *for narrow character string parameters*

86. *Pass enumerator values, not integer constants*

87. *Do not use* void* *in a public interface*

88. *Use inline functions instead of macros*

89. *Inline only the simplest of functions*

90. *Factor functions to allow inlining of trivial cases*

91. *Define small classes and small methods*

92. *Build fundamental classes from standard types*

93. *Avoid the use of virtual base classes in user-extensible class hierarchies*

94. *Declare the access level of all members*

95. *Declare all member variables private*

96. *Avoid the use of friend declarations*

97. *Declare an explicit default constructor for added clarity*

98. *Always declare a copy constructor, assignment operator, and destructor if the class can be instantiated*

99. *Always implement a virtual destructor if your class may be subclassed*

100. *Make constructors protected to prohibit direct instantiation*

101. *Make constructors private to prohibit derivation*

102. *Declare a private* `operator new()` *to prohibit dynamic allocation*

103. *Declare a protected or private destructor to prohibit static or automatic allocation*

104. *Declare single-parameter constructors as* `explicit` *to avoid unexpected type conversions*

105. *Use default arguments to reduce the number of constructors*

106. *Do not overload non-virtual methods in subclasses*

107. *Declare virtual methods protected and call them from public non-virtual methods*

108. *Keep your functions "const-correct"*

109. *Use object pointers and references in class declarations*

150. *Always code a* break *statement in the last case of a switch statement*

151. *Use return codes to report expected state changes*

152. *Use assertions to enforce a programming contract*

153. *Do not silently absorb or ignore unexpected runtime errors*

154. *Use assertions to report unexpected or unhandled runtime errors*

155. *Use exceptions to report errors that may occur under normal program execution*

156. *Manage resources with RAII for exception safety*

157. *Catch exceptions by reference, not by value*

158. *Do not discard exception information if you throw a new exception within a* catch *block*

159. *Avoid throwing exceptions in destructors*

160. *Use lazy evaluation and initialization*

161. *Reuse objects to avoid reallocation*

162. *Leave optimization for last*

8. Packaging Conventions

163. *Use unnamed namespaces instead of* static *to hide local functions and variables*

164. *Tread lightly on the global namespace*

165. *Place types that are commonly used, changed, and released together, or mutually dependent on each other, into the same package*

166. *Isolate unstable classes in separate packages*

167. *Avoid making difficult-to-change packages dependent on packages that are easy to change*

168. *Maximize abstraction to maximize stability*

169. *Capture high-level design and architecture as stable abstractions organized into stable packages*

170. *Use the class name as the filename*

171. *Use separate files for each namespace-scope* class, struct, union, enumeration, *function, or overloaded function group*

172. *Use* #include *sparingly in header files*

173. *Implement class methods outside of their class declaration block*

174. *Do not name files containing tests or examples the same as template header file names*

175. *Do not put global-scope* using *or* using namespace *declarations in a header file*

Glossary

abstract class
A class that exists only as a superclass of another class and can never be directly instantiated.

abstract data type
Defines a type that may have many implementations. Abstract data types encapsulate data with operations on that data such that the user of the type need not be concerned with the implementation. Abstract data types include things like dates, strings, stacks, queues, and trees.

abstract method
A method that has no implementation. Also known as a "pure virtual" method; this method must be overridden in derived classes to be used.

abstract type
Defines the type for a set of objects, where each object must also belong to a set of objects that conform to a known subtype of the abstract type. An abstract type may have one or more implementations.

abstraction
The process and result of extracting the common or general characteristics from a set of similar entities.

accessor
A method that gets the value of an object member variable.

active object
An object that possesses its own thread of control.

acyclic dependency
   A dependency relationship where one entity has a direct or indirect dependency on a second entity, but the second entity has no direct or indirect dependency on the first.

aggregation
   An association representing a whole–part containment relationship.

architecture
   A description of the organization and structure of a software system.

argument
   Data item bound to a parameter in a method call.

assertion
   A statement about the truth of a logical expression.

attribute
   A named characteristic or property of a type, class, or object.

behavior
   The activities and effects produced by an object in response to an event or method call.

binary compatible
   A situation where one version of a software component may be directly and transparently substituted for another version of that component without recompiling the component's clients.

block statement
   The C++ language construct that combines one or more statement expressions into a single compound statement, by enclosing them in curly braces: "{...}".

built-in type
   A data type defined as part of the language. The built-in or native types defined by C++ include bool, the signed and

unsigned integer types, char, short, int and long, the floating point types float and double, and the unspecific type void.

class
A user-defined type.

class hierarchy
A set of classes associated by inheritance relationships.

client
An entity that requests a service from another entity.

cohesion
The degree to which two or more entities belong together or relate to each other.

component
A physical and discrete software entity that conforms to a set of interfaces.

composition
A form of aggregation where an object is composed of other objects.

concrete class
A completely specified class that may be directly instantiated. A concrete class defines a specific implementation for an abstract class or type.

concrete type
A type that may be directly instantiated. A concrete type may refine or extend an abstract type.

concurrency
The degree by which two or more activities (threads of execution) occur or make progress at the same time.

constraint
A restriction on the value or behavior of an entity.

constructor

A special method that initializes a new instance of a class.

container

An object whose purpose is to contain and manipulate other objects.

contract

A clear description of the responsibilities and constraints that apply between a client and a type, class, or method.

coupling

The degree to which two or more entities are dependent on each other.

critical section

A block of code that allows only one thread at a time to enter and execute the instructions within that block. Any threads attempting to enter a critical section while another thread is already executing within that section are blocked until the original thread exits.

cyclic dependency

A dependency relationship where one entity has a direct or indirect dependency on a second entity and the second entity also has a direct or indirect dependency on the first.

data type

A primitive or built-in type that represents pure data and has no distinct identity as an object.

delegation

The act of passing a message, and responsibility, from one object to a second object to elicit a desired response.

dependency

A relationship where the semantic characteristics of one entity rely upon and constrain the semantic characteristics of another entity.

derivation
The process of defining a new type or class by specializing or extending the behavior and attributes of an existing type or class.

domain
An area of expertise, knowledge, or activity.

encapsulation
The degree to which an appropriate mechanism hides the internal data, structure, and implementation of an object or other entity.

enumeration
A type that defines a list of named values that make up the allowable range for values of that type.

factor
The act of reorganizing one or more types or classes by extracting responsibilities from existing classes and synthesizing new classes to handle these responsibilities.

field
An instance variable or data member of an object.

fundamental data type
A type that typically requires only one implementation and is commonly used to construct other, more useful, types. Dates, complex numbers, linked lists, and vectors are examples of common fundamental data types.

generalization
The process of extracting the common or general characteristics from a set of similar entities to create a new entity that possesses these common characteristics.

implementation
The concrete realization of a contract defined by a type, abstract class, or interface. The actual code.

implementation class

A concrete class that provides an implementation for a type, abstract class, or interface.

implementation inheritance

The action or mechanism by which a subclass inherits the implementation and interface from one or more super-classes.

inheritance

The mechanism by which more specialized entities acquire or incorporate the responsibilities or implementation of more generalized entities.

instance

The result of instantiating a class—the concrete representation of an object.

instantiation

The action or mechanism by which a type or class is reified to create an actual object. The act of allocating and initializing an object from a class.

interface

The methods exposed by a type, class, or object. Also a set of operations that define an abstract service.

invariant

An expression that describes the well-defined, legal states of an object.

keyword

A language construct. Keywords are reserved and cannot be used as identifiers.

lazy evaluation

When an implementation delays the evaluation of an expression until the last possible moment. With respect to object lifetimes, this can mean delaying object construction and initialization until the object is actually required.

The intent is to gain efficiency by avoiding unnecessary work.

local variable
A variable that is automatically allocated and initialized on the call "stack." Includes parameter variables that are bound to function arguments.

method
The implementation of an operation. An operation defined by an interface or class.

multiple inheritance
Inheritance relationship where a subtype inherits from two or more supertypes.

mutator
A method that sets the value of an object member variable.

mutex
A synchronization mechanism used to provide mutually exclusive access to a resource. A mutex is generally used to serialize access to a critical section. See **critical section**.

native type
See **built-in type**.

nested class
A class defined within the scope of another class.

object
The result of instantiating a class. An entity with state, behavior, and identity.

operation
A service that may be requested from an object to effect behavior. Alternatively viewed as a message sent from a client to an object.

package
A mechanism organizing and naming a collection of related classes.

parameter

A variable that is bound to an argument value passed into a method.

polymorphic

A method that can operate correctly on a variety of types. Also, a trait or characteristic of an object whereby that object can appear as several different types at the same time.

polymorphism

The concept or mechanism by which objects of different types inherit the responsibility for implementing the same operation, but respond differently to the invocation of that operation.

postcondition

A constraint or assertion that must hold true following the completion of an operation.

precondition

A constraint or assertion that must hold true at the start of an operation.

primitive type

See **built-in type**.

private access

An access-control characteristic applied to class inheritance relationships and class members. Class members declared with the `private` access modifier are only accessible to code in the same class and are not inherited by subclasses.

property

A named characteristic or attribute of a type, class, or object.

protected access

An access-control characteristic applied to class inheritance relationships and class members. Class members declared with the `protected` access modifier are accessible to code in the same class and are inherited by subclasses.

public access

An access-control characteristic applied to class inheritance relationships and class members. Class members declared with the public access modifier are accessible anywhere the class is accessible and are inherited by subclasses.

qualifier

A name or value used to locate or identify a particular entity within a set of similar entities.

realization

A relationship where one entity abides by or the contract specified by another entity.

responsibility

A purpose or obligation assigned to a type.

role

The set of responsibilities associated with an entity that participates in a specific relationship.

serialization

The process of granting a single thread access to a critical section while blocking all other threads. Serialization is usually synonymous with synchronization. See **synchronization** and **critical section**.

service

One or more operations provided by a type, class, or object to accomplish useful work on behalf of one or more clients.

signature

The name and parameter types associated with an operation.

state

The condition or value of an object.

static type checking

Compile-time verification of the assumptions made about the use of object reference and data value types.

subclass

A class that inherits attributes and methods from another class.

subtype

The more specific type in a specialization–generalization relationship.

superclass

A class from which a subclass inherits attributes and methods.

supertype

The more general type in a specialization–generalization relationship.

synchronization

The process or mechanism used to preserve the invariant states of a program or object in the presence of multiple threads. See **serialization** and **critical section**.

thread

A single flow of control within a process that executes a sequence of instructions in an independent execution context.

type

Defines the common responsibilities, behavior, and operations associated with a set of similar objects. A type does not define an implementation.

variable

A typed, named container for holding object references or data values.

visibility

The degree to which an entity may be accessed from outside of a particular scope.

Bibliography

Brackett, George. "Class 6: Designing for Communication: Layout, Structure, Navigation for Nets and Webs." In "Course T525: Designing Educational Experiences for Networks and Webs." (Harvard Graduate School of Education, 26 August 1999).

Cargill, Tom. "C++ Gotchas: Tutorial Notes." p. 13. Distributed at these seminars: http://www.profcon.com/profcon/Gotchas.htm

Dijkstra, Edsger W. "Go To Statement Considered Harmful," Communications of the ACM, Vol. 11, No. 3 (Mar 1968), pp. 147–148.

Gamma, Eric et al. *Design Patterns: Elements of Reusable Object-Oriented Software*. (Reading, Massachusetts: Addison-Wesley, 1995), pp. 325–330.

Karabatsos, Jim. "When does this document apply?" In "Visual Basic Programming Standards." (GUI Computing Ltd., 22 Mar 1996).

Kernighan, Brian, and P. J. Plauger. *The Elements of Programming Style*. (New York: McGraw-Hill, 1988), p. 118.

Lea, Doug. *Concurrent Programming in Java*TM: *Design Principles and Patterns*. (Reading, Massachusetts: Addison-Wesley, 1997), pp. 1–2.

Liskov, Barbara, and Guttag, John. *Abstraction and Specification in Program Development*. (New York: McGraw-Hill, 1986).

Martin, Robert. "Engineering Notebook: The Open-Closed Principle," C++ Report, Vol. 8, No. 1 (Jan 1996).

Martin, Robert. "Engineering Notebook," C++ Report, Vol. 8, No. 3 (Mar 1996).

Martin, Robert. "Engineering Notebook: Granularity," C++ Report, Vol. 8, No. 10 (Nov 1996), pp. 57–62.

Martin, Robert. "Engineering Notebook: Stability," C++ Report, Vol. 9, No. 2 (Feb 1997).

McConnell, Steve. *Code Complete*. (Redmond, Washington: Microsoft Press, 1993), pp. 337–338.

Meyer, Bertrand. *Object-Oriented Software Construction*. (Englewood Cliffs, New Jersey: Prentice Hall, 2000).

Meyers, Scott. *More Effective C++*. (Reading, Massachusetts: Addison-Wesley, 1996), pp. 35–38.

Meyers, Scott. *Effective C++: 50 Specific Ways to Improve Your Programs and Design, Second Edition*. (Reading, Massachusetts. Addison-Wesley, 1997), p. 16.

Schmidt, Douglas C., and Harrison, Tim. *Pattern Languages of Program Design*. (Reading, Massachusetts: Addison-Wesley, 1997).

Stroustrup, Bjarne. *The Design and Evolution of C++*. (Reading, Massachusetts: Addison-Wesley, 1994).

Stroustrup, Bjarne. *The C++ Programming Language, Third Edition*. (Reading, Massachusetts: Addison-Wesley, 1997).

Index